Between Women, Friends or Enemies?

Gladys Morales-Smith

Between Women, Friends or Enemies?

Gladys Morales-Smith

Dedication

To Richard, my husband, my love, friend and companion. My mother Aurora and Hector my father, both with love and dedication taught me to pursue my dreams. My mother's parents, Margarita (Mamaita), a wise and wonderful grandma, and Arnaldo (Nono) my grandpa who loved to spoil my sisters and me. Their unconditional love has been my inspiration to look for a world of equality where women and men build a more just and egalitarian society.

Between Women, Friends or Enemies?

Also, special thanks to Darcy S. English, my sister in law, for assisting me in translating this book into English

Gladys Morales-Smith

Table of Contents

Between Women, Friends or Enemies?

Gladys Morales-Smith

Gladys Morales-Smith

Introduction

The efforts of women for recognition of their rights for the past 150 years have made possible a larger and more dynamic presence of females in all levels of modern society. Especially in the work place, women have advanced to a great extent thanks to laws and recognition of their abilities and efforts in the international community. An important milestone was The United Nations meeting in 1975 when representatives from all over the world agreed to adopt more laws to recognize and improve the role of women in modern society. Unfortunately the same females who with their behavior are usually competitive, defensive and often show lack of solidarity often overshadow those advances. Especially in the work place where they create an adverse environment , which ultimately affects productivity and harmony either at the office, an industrial field or a government institution. In the social sphere, that destructive competition is reflected in irrational actions where instead of uniting for a common cause they always are in conflict. Family life is another area where relations of women often are devastating for the harmony and development of family, which is the basic core of society as a whole.

1

Between Women, Friends or Enemies?

This book is the result of many years of research and a lifetime of experiences as a woman, journalist and diplomat in diverse work places and countries. As a scholar of the status of women, I have always been observing the female behavior at home, work, and the environment in general. Women mostly are more competitive among themselves, and unlike them females fail to maintain a basic level of solidarity and respect between themselves.

Therefore, the effort to present this work responds to the necessity of solutions for a better understanding of the subject and to foster in women a serious reflection about the negative behavior they develop, and the terrible effects caused by them. This behavior limits the progress of females and, ultimately, contributes to many of the problems of modern society.

In the course of this book, alternatives to change the existing situation are offered. Also, it inspires to seek contributions of women to society in a positive way. In addition, guidelines to behave with solidarity between women and, while keeping the respect to the individuality and ability of recognition of the best of other females. Practicing this line of thought will multiply women's contribution towards a more just and harmonious world.

Realistically, women, with exceptions, have not made a substantial change in human relationships until today. I believe this is the result of many variables that contribute to this self-destructive attitude where the media have played an important role in molding a distorted image of what it means to treat other woman equally and at the same time be an independent female, and respect the fruit of struggles and efforts of millions of women in the past. On the contrary, the media spreads patterns where narcissism, selfishness, confrontation, competition and disloyalty, among others, are the features that nurture the inspiration of the women of the 21st century. Most of the reality shows fall into this category and encourage this destructive relation between women.

In this sense, it is appropriate to draw this to the attention of women. Then they can have a positive attitude and better self-esteem and can start changing the inappropriate idea of what until now, it means to be a real liberated, independent, and fraternal woman.

Thus, this book evaluates the situation in which we live, and gives guidelines to eradicate this negative image of women in the home, work place and every day life in general.

Between Women; Friends or Enemies? recognizes and points out that even though manuals have been written in the past, giving tips on how to behave well in "society", in order to create a more harmonious environment; unfortunately, they did not address directly the good manners between women. The absence or very little existence of harmonious patterns of behavior between females has been taken as normal. And, if there is not a frame of reference, it is assumed they do not need to feel remorse when they damage or fail to show respect for another women, or if they are always in conflict between themselves. As a result, there has not been enough progress gained in spite of women having more access to education, to work, or to political power, because in essence, they still maintain the perception of society in an uneven manner in terms of dealing with other women and also, in the way how they treat men. In this sense it is still common to see women with power being abusive with her peers and acting submissive with men.

Furthermore, the goal of this book is also assessing how the language, fashion, education, heritage of traditions and myths make it more difficult to get rid of this kind of behavior of the majority of women in modern society. Therefore women should carefully consider how to talk, how to dress, communicate with their behavior, and how to interact in the surroundings in which they live.

Also, it is the purpose of this book to bring attention about laws that increase women's share of the labor force that are overshadowed when the supposed beneficiaries (women), instead of working towards a common goal squander their energies on futile clashes between themselves. More so, how productivity and the image of an institution are affected by the attitude of many women who carry to their work places prejudices that they have been raised with in their families and environment. Thus, offices or work places become battlegrounds where the confrontation and lost of efforts take precedence. In countries like Canada or the United States the issue has caught the attention of labor authorities, and they are carrying out studies where they are looking for reasons and solutions to make women more professional when dealing with themselves, and avoid sabotage to the work of their peers with inappropriate behavior.

Through this book, readers may have a broader vision of what it means to be a woman in the 21st century. And, by utilizing the suggestions offered in this book, they will contribute to banish irregular behaviors, as well as fruitless confrontations between women, which continues to limit them in the achievement of the common goal, which is a better and more equitable world.

In summary, the knowledge of our self-esteem and us depend on being taken seriously and with respect. Consequently, one of the reasons for writing this book is to draw attention to a situation that not only hurts women, but society in general. Thus its contribution to offer guidelines and a framework to change the unnecessary aggression practiced between women.

Chapter 1

Are There Good Manners Between Women?

According to my observations most women do not treat other woman with proper manners. It appears there are few written or oral examples, which establish guidelines that serve as a frame of reference for the way women treat each other. It is good to remember that the topic of good manners has been and, is to this day, underestimated and is assigned as merely a superficial meaning. Good manners throughout history have shown their positive influence to human behavior, which is fundamental in the harmonious development of a society as a whole. Specifically between women, good manners have been almost ignored which has deepened the traditional problems of integration of females to society. Today, with the increase of women in the workforce, the rise of abuse between women, (especially at work), worries authorities in the government and entrepreneurs of the private sector; so good manners between women is a current and urgent theme to be researched by experts. The problem is serious and has very deep roots.

Historically women's relations have been portrayed with lack of empathy, unhealthy competition and confrontation as their main ingredients. There are few records of cases where two women are supported by each other, or reflect confidence in their peers. And, if there were exceptions, they have been forgotten. On the other hand, history is full of cases of suspicion, infidelity, and betrayal as common features in the relationships of women. Now, new generations with all the accomplishments still maintain those old and questionable patterns of behavior between themselves.

It is difficult to determine how to change the traditional attitudes, which divide and destroy efforts of females, and promote the flourishing of harmonious and equitable behavior between women in society. I believe in order to succeed it requires greater gender awareness based on adequate information as well as substantive changes of ancient attitudes. Those ones have only managed to deepen the traditional female problems, as well as difficulties in the world in general. Therefore, a new way of behavior between women will be the initial step to achieve goals included into laws and international agreements favoring equality and universal justice.

Gladys Morales-Smith

It needs to be recognized that in the world of the early 21st century, women still have attitudes and ways of life very at odds with the respect of themselves as human beings. So, when it comes to dealing with other women, especially when a common interest brings them together, which could be work, family ties or the dispute over a man; confrontation is the main ingredient in their relations. For this reason, the importance of friendly and harmonious treatment is the basic natural rule that needs to be exercised between them. But is that possible? Yes, I believe it is, as long as women can develop higher self-esteem, which is reflected in the respect of their peers.

Chapter 2

Some History of Courtesy and Etiquette

In everyday language, the term etiquette has been identified as a set of rules and practices that establishes courteous manners in our relationship with others. And, etiquette has determined behaviors aimed to give some uniformity to basic concepts that characterize interpersonal relations. In this line of thinking, it is important to mention the Spanish term, "cortesía", defined as the appropriate behavior among peers of the same sex. Due to the patriarchal origins of Spanish language this term is assigned primarily to men but not to women. So, language has a direct influence in the behavior between women. (Courtesy, Gender and Language, Chapter 6)

It is appropriate to mention that the term etiquette, which has been identified with the practice of good manners, is derived from the French word "etiquette" which means sign or notice .The term refers to the habit started at the beginning of the European monarchies when, at the entrance of the palaces there was a notice specifying the clothing to wear for the occasion and who was invited to the event. Today the meaning of etiquette is much broader.

Specifically, the origins of the term date back to the reign of Louis XIV in France, who established the custom of placing a poster(etiquette) stating the rules to be followed by the guests during the events convened by the king and his court. Thus this custom spread to certain basic forms of behavior in social gatherings, which denoted the existence of a social class "above the common people". Subsequently, in the 19th-century the Industrial Revolution in the United States and England originated the flourishing of large cities where social dynamics brought new members to the economically more privileged class. These newcomers needed advice on how to integrate into the traditional elite (old money) in their environment. In the United States, for example, a wave of European immigrants of modest resources ascended socially thanks to their success in business, but these "new rich" lacked knowledge regarding behavior and social relations. Such situations gave rise to the proliferation of manuals written by both men and women trying to say what was or was not appropriate for entry into the upper levels of their social circumstances. An example of such a statement is a summary of the following Prologue from "Manual of Etiquette" by Daisy Eyebright in 1897.

Between Women, Friends or Enemies?

"These pages have been prepared for those who seek self-assurance in their external appearance and want to increase their knowledge about issues of social relations. It has not been written for those who have been trained in the best use of the society from their childhood; not for those who have learned good manners at the same time as the alphabet, but for those, from both sexes, less fortunate in our land; those who are eager to gain a knowledge of etiquette that governs social relations and they are eager to cultivate themselves in the practice and use of good manners".

An international example is the "Manual of Carreño", which is similar to "Etiquette. The Blue Book of Social Usage", by Emily Post in the United States. The original title of this Venezuelan author was: "Handbook of Civility and Good Manners for Use of the Youth of Both Sexes in which are the Main Rules of Civility and Etiquette that Should Be Observed in Different Social Situations", this book was published in 1853 by the Venezuelan educator Manuel Antonio Carreño. In this manual - widely accepted in Latin America-, Carreño repeats the traditional concepts of similar Europeans or Americans authors. It is interesting to remark that the long title of the book mentions "youth of both sexes", probably taking into account his daughter, the famous pianist Teresa Carreño whom the educator and author dedicated much of his life to promoting her artistic qualities internationally.

In the United States, the 20th century was marked by Emily Post's book, "Etiquette", "The Blue Book of Social Usage", published for the first time in 1922. Post, in her first chapter states "The true meaning of etiquette ... As a mater of fact, there is no one single thing that we do, or say, or choose, or use, or even think that does not follow (or break) one of the exactions of taste, or tact, or ethics, or good manners, or etiquette – call it what you will."

Also, it is appropriate to mention that in spite of given a superficial connotation to the issue of politeness, this way of behavior has allowed the development of harmonious relations in society, which is a basic requirement for implementation and success of fair and equitable policies between men and women in any society. Because, starting with simple logical thinking, how can the laws that protect women be respected, if the beneficiaries are not looking at themselves as human beings that are worthy, and deserve respect and equal treatment? Courtesy and good treatment between individuals without distinction of sex is a cornerstone in any society seeking justice and equality.

These historical issues about good manners (in the 19th and 20th centuries) were usually related to emerging elites, and the manuals about this matter also encouraged typical or traditional behaviors in relation to gender. These publications usually referred to the "proper" behavior of the male or the female in relation to his/her opposite gender. Thus it was said for example " a lady can not speak about this or that subject in front of a male". Rarely or almost never was their advise as to how woman should treat each other as friends, colleagues at work or as a relative. Feminist movements in the 19th and 20th centuries brought new questions, emphasizing the male-female relationship, but not those between women. It should not be ignored that progress was made in terms of creation of feminist organizations seeking common objectives for a better treatment from society towards females. But many women forgot how to treat each other. It is undeniable that women in the last century; more aware of their essence and reality, have shown progress but I believe, those advances have been very few. Because of this situation, the need arises to seek new models of women who can develop a more caring attitude and with a broader vision of their role in society, only then can there be more equitable and therefore fairer societies.

Chapter 3

Women As Agents For Change

Concept of gender

In spite of wide acceptance of the basic concept of equality of human beings without distinction of any kind; the contemporary world faces a severe crisis of gender identity. And, it is mainly because how modern media stereotypes the roles of men and women. Those with different options that existed in our societies since ancient times are not the total answer to a series of ways of behavior related to hormonal development of the individual. Advocates of alternative options of gender behavior questioned cultural and biological traditional concepts without proving a hundred percent their new theories that defend most behaviors are based on cultural influences.

Between Women, Friends or Enemies?

It is disturbing to note how individuals who do not match within the commonly accepted gender profile create different justifications to their status and seek to minimize the importance of the definition of gender in the modern society. In this game, the woman loses her individual identity because in many cases her distinctiveness is distorted in order to justify the presence of trans genders. This creates a whole mode of behavior that is now being evaluated by scientists from different disciplines.

There are examples in recent history, like the one that occurred in the middle of the last century in which a trend started intended to demonstrate that the behavior of the male or the female corresponded to models created by society. A New Zealand psychologist, John Monney was an advocate of this theory. According to him, someone who was born male could become female after treatment. The famous case John and Joan (a boy who was castrated by a medical error during his circumcision), which Dr. Monney alluded as his masterpiece was discovered as a failure a few years ago and proved that the child, despite the psychological and hormonal treatments never doubted and defended his condition as a male.

These cases that occurred by the hundreds in several countries of the Northern hemisphere, especially in the United States, demonstrated the complexity of the issue and the need to recognize the importance of the definition of gender within the world in which we live. It is also appropriate o mention recent occurrences where parents decide to ignore the sex of their child so the child will be raised without gender imposition by the society.

All of this is respectable, but it goes against the sexual identity of the individual when his/her biological gender is ignored. The matter is not to ignore or respect other types of behavior, what remains clear is that biologically there are two genders that are in correspondence to their genetic composition: female and male gender. In this sense the interest is focusing on the role of the female element, her behavior and advances as agent for change.

On the other hand, these changes of behavior cannot be ignored. In countries like Argentina and Uruguay already new laws have given to a person the decision of what gender they want to be, and thus his/her identification document stipulates it, regardless of their biological sex. In other words, trans genders are recognized and are given the option to define the gender that frames his/her behavior in society.

The Journal of the Office of the Special Adviser on Gender and Advancement of Women (United Nations, August 2001) refers to the concept of gender as: "Social differences incurred by attributes and opportunities associated with being female or male and interactions and social relations between men and women. Gender determines what is expected, enables and develops in a woman and man within a given context. In most societies, there are differences and inequalities between women and men within the roles and responsibilities

11

assigned, activities taken, access to and control over resources, as well as opportunities to decide..."

This context includes concepts such as gender equality in the sense of providing equal opportunities for all members of society. The main stream of gender has been defined by the United Nations as: "the process of rating implications for women and men because of a planned action, including legislation, policies or programs, in any area and at all levels. It is a strategy for making the concerns and experiences of women, like men, a design with integral dimension, implementation, monitoring, and evaluation of policies and programs in all political, economic and social spheres, so that women and men benefit equally and inequality is not perpetuated. "The ultimate goal of gender mainstream is to achieve equality of gender..."

The inclusion of these ideas is important because they make us aware of the concepts related to equality, and access to better opportunities in life. These theories are important for the development of just and harmonious societies. Thus, the woman who is aware of her gender identity makes it possible to be an agent of change towards better society. If by the contrary, a woman ignores her essence and role in her surroundings it will be difficult for her to understand her role in modern society. Numbers and percentages are a frame of reference, but they do not reflect the total history of a specific reality. For example, we can say there are now a higher percentage of women in the work force, but how they are treated and how they deal with each other is the most important thing if you look for the genuine harmonious development of a society.

On the other hand, when referring to the presence of women in higher levels of power, their progress should not be based only on reviewing statistics. If, for example, there is a fifty percent work force comprised of women in the public administration, and many of them have achieved power by questionable ways (making use of their attributes, relations and physical favors); then the presence of that portion –big or small- has no value whatsoever. If by the contrary, women with special skills and knowledge are recognized in their environment and have important positions, then the progress is obvious. In summary, the statistics help to get an idea of a reality, but do not fully reflect the total social effects that it is intended to study or evaluate.

Currently, there exists a type of woman, present in different levels of society, but alien to the changes needed to make a modern society where justice and social welfare are guaranteed. Also, many women have come to power and have followed the same levels of corruption as their male predecessors. In other words, women's' role as agent for change has not been completed. Why? There are many reasons, one of them, perhaps the main one is the lack of authentic solidarity with other women due to their ignorance or indifference of

their role in a society that is looking for real change.

Chapter 4

How do Women See and Treat Each Other?

It can be seen very far back in history the ways women treated each other as can be seen in this example the letter from the Duchess of Orleans to Duchess of Hanover. January 4, 1704. Versailles, France.

"I must tell you how just the king is. The Duchesse de Bourgogne, ladies who are called "Ladies of the Palace", tried to arrogate the rank and take the place of my ladies everywhere. Such a thing was never done either in the time of the Queen or the Dauphiness. They got the King's Guards to keep on their places and push back the chairs belonging my ladies. I complaint first was to the Duc of Noailles, who replied that it was the King's order. Then I went immediately and said to him. "I ask our Majesty if it is by your orders that my ladies have now no place or rank as they use to have? If it is your desire, I have nothing more to say, because I only wish to obey you, but your Majesty knows that formerly when the Queen and the Dauphiness were alive the ladies of the Palace had no rank, and my Maids of Honor, Gentlemen of honor, and Ladies of the Robe had their places like those of the Queen and the Dauphiness. I do not know why the Ladies of the Palace should pretend to anything else". The King became quite red and replied, "I have given no such order, who said that I had? "The Marechal de Noailles, I replied. The King asked him why he had said such a thing, and he denied it entirely. "I am willing to believe, since you say so" I replied, "that my lackey misunderstood you, but as the King has given no such orders, see that your Guards don't keep places for those ladies and hinder my servants from carrying chairs for my service as we say here. Although these are high in favor of the King, nevertheless, sent the majordomo to find out how things should be done. I told him " These women are becoming far to insolent now that they are in favor of the King and they imagined that I would not have the courage to report the matter to the King. But I shall not lose my rank nor prerogatives on account of the favor they enjoyed. The King is too just for that. (G.S. Stevenson, ed. The Letters of Madame, (New York. 1924), pp. 232-233.

The incident where the Duchess of Orleans comments to her peer from Hanover, denotes how rivalry has been and is until today, the main ingredient in woman's relations and the dispute for the favor of a man is often the most common cause of confrontation. Also, it demonstrates how women try to undermine or defame someone (usually another woman) who is absent during the exchange or conversation. And, this is not an isolated case.

The confrontation between women is a common feature and reflects the misrepresented and contested concept derived from the book "The Prince" of Machiavelli: "Divide and Conquer". The motto seems to be, while women are more divided, it will be easier to subdue them.

Unfortunately this goal is facilitated if adding confrontation usually disguised as supposed competition, as has been the trend in the relationships of women according to documents and letters found from the past. But is that the whole truth or part of it? Always, or almost always, "they" (women) have seen each other from levels, for example they acted with prejudice of superiority as some forms of relationship. Almost always women can not see themselves as equals like from a perspective of sisterhood, as it occurs to a greater extent among men (brotherhood). For women the word solidarity has mostly a discriminatory connotation and selfish characteristic and seldom applies their solidarity to a wide range of similar of the same sex.

In the historical books concerning famous women they corroborate that most of the time females are described as egocentric and share little friendship with other women. There is very little documentation concerning the existence of fraternal relationships between women. On the contrary, many cases of infamy and confrontation between them are highlighted. Among the traitors, if there was a woman then the common reason was the conquests or to   gain the favors of a man. That was the role that was assigned to the women which reduces them to a kind of being that not deserve respect in society. It should be remembered that in Ancient Greece, the philosopher Aristotle considered friendship between women was not possible due to " their lack of spirituality and loyalty assigned only to men". (Books VIII and IX of the Ethics).

But is this condition true or invented intentionally to justify oppression and omission of females in development of history? Women in power have often been abusive with members of the same gender. Is it because lack of experience, reaction to oppression or exaggeration of the history? Doubt remains, if it is undeniable that probably some women imitated men's abusive behavior, it is hard to believe that all women in power had the same conduct. In other words according to the way history as it is written does not help to shape a real view of women from the past.

The question still can be asked is how women see each other? Events of the last two centuries show that the suffragette movements in the 19th Century and feminists of the past 100 years have slowly influenced the change of the image of women in history. In the mid-20th century when a new generation of women such as Simone de Beauvoir have challenged the status of women and their historical treatment with her book "The Second Sex", (1948). The second wave of feminists around the world that followed her line of thinking reached a more substantive change for the benefit of females. The result was undoubtedly a different type of woman: with more self-awareness, more confidence and more acceptances in the work place. The interrogation that first arises facing all this progress is: with all the advances of the past century, do women really respect each other? Are they indeed agents for change with a greater capacity of organization and decision making so that preparing society for a better place for future generations? It seems not enough progress has been made. And we ask again, why so little? Maybe simply because the vision of women themselves have not really changed enough to respect each other, and therefore there is not significant overall respect for themselves and their efforts in modern society.

In recent years with more women in power a negative behavior between them can still sometimes be seen. Females still have the tendency to distrust each other, even at levels where the education and awareness of their role in society are not in doubt.

But that is not all of the reality. The Presidents of Argentina and Brazil, Cristina Fernández Kirchner and Dilma Rousseff, respectively, are teaching professionalism and true consciousness of being women as agents of change. In their performance and especially in bilateral meetings they show a courteous and fraternal relationship between them. According to the little information given by the media, both women develop agendas related to their countries and put into practice their policies characterized by the search for the common good of their citizens. It is necessary to say that both Chiefs of State have developed a long and active political life before they took their positions. President Fernández de Kirchner has worked as a lawyer at different public offices in Argentina and, as the wife of her late husband (ex President Nestor Kirchner), she was very actively involved in promoting laws that changed the situation of poverty and inequality of the majority of people in her country.

In Brazil, President Dilma Rousseff is an economist with a long career in the public administration. She has been Minister and Head of the Cabinet of ex President Luis Ignacio da Silva, (Lula), before becoming the first woman president in her country. Ms. Rousseff also has a long political history, which denotes her concern for social justice and a substantial change in the political and economic rules in Brazil, in order to achieve a qualitative step forward in her country.

Presidents Kirchner and Rousseff are aware of their reality and are committed to it; and they also are demonstrating their ability to strengthen ties between their countries. This fact is unprecedented and carries large and positive implications for the region, if we take into consideration that Argentina and Brazil are the two largest nations of South America.

Even though there are cases where women forget their role as agents of change once in power, there are positive cases as examples mentioned above. And these cases are the ones that should be widely spread and used as models to be followed by new generations of women.

There are still numerous cases where a woman, after achieving a position of power, develops an attitude where other women are targets of her abuse of power. Those attitudes reflect how little progress has been made regarding respect for their fellow females. Especially in cases where females may state they are advocates of women's rights, but in practice they do not recognize them with respect or intend to do so.

Chapter 5

Etiquette Used as an Instrument to Maintain Traditional Roles

In recent years the financial and cultural globalization process has been a large influence in the consideration of etiquette as an important subject. This wave contains the risk of perpetuating roles not so different from the patterns of old behavior. Therefore, while certain changes introduced into the business protocol recognize the presence of women, in essence there still persists certain situations and circumstances that may well affect the role of women in the future of society. The international protocol still maintains exclusive roles for a man or less attention for a woman. For example, sometimes if there is a high executive woman, she is not treated as a man's equal in her position, which still reflects the slow change towards equal treatment to women also in the business world.

Let us remember that, following royal rules from the past, women used to play a decorative role. They were appreciated for their beauty, exuberance in their dress, use of jewels, makeup, and their capacity of the conquest of men rather than their intellectual ability. Also, they were recognized for developing good relations with people and the capacity to maintain harmonious relations in their environment. Even today many women in politics or public administration still play this role, in many instances that reflects there are not major changes in society.

The excess of attention to women's' external characteristics from the past was somewhat overshadowed with the feminist movements of the 20th century, especially in the decades of the 1960's and 1970's. During those years, new women's' behavior patterns arose. Less adjusted to the new roles, the relationship between them also changed and it was given greater importance to the relationship within the female group. Also women had better education and knowledge of their role as a woman and they were also questioning their role in society and rejecting behaviors that denigrate women in society. The mobilization emerged naturally from the grassroots movements.

Quickly, in the middle of the seventies, "the establishment" systematically redirected the movement through international meetings and agencies that supposedly were going to revalue women in society. It is important to recognize that with these efforts a process of evaluation of women's contribution was initiated in societies around the world. Then, on the other hand, those efforts have been given from the top to the bottom of society eclipsing the natural process of change that must arise from the very foundations of the interested groups. Thus, the reason most females today think that laws and quotas for integration are something natural and not the result of centuries of struggle for basic rights. And, it is undeniable that differences in treatment in the working world among men and women continue to be part of the problem. These are isolated cases and not a new orientation where women have a different role in society and with innovative solutions to problems of centuries. The pattern of behavior continues prioritizing women in relation to men; there is not a substantive change. Men, from their side, apparently, have more solidarity between themselves regardless of culture or ethnicity. This is not the case between women.

It is also noticed when females advance politically, for instance in positions of power, they show traditional attitudes of men in terms of their relationship with other women and with men. The model of "Queen Bee" is very common. Also, in the work place it is common to find something, which is the subtle manipulation of the concept of women as objects. These situations reaffirm how little progress has been made towards a new form of acceptance of women based on their merits and integration into society and the business world.

Of course there are exceptions to the rule, and that is what should be taken as models to be spread in order to promote more just and equitable societies. The idea is that courtesy, proper treatment and good manners, not only fits for both sexes but between women, especially in every moment of their life (home, work and society in general). Recently, in the last presidential election, an adviser to the United States President Barack Obama, referred disparagingly about the wife of an opposite presidential candidate. The comment referred to the fact that the candidate's wife had never worked and, as a consequence, she had no experience to speak about labor issues. The adviser either ignored or downplayed the view of the opponent because she had never worked outside the home and had only exercised the role of a homemaker. This attitude is very common between women because many of them consider that only working at home has no significance or economic value because there is no monetary compensation. It is nothing further from the truth. The role of the majority of females at home is invaluable and vital in the family. It is a choice of life that must be respected. These mistaken concepts reflect once again the serious problem that exists between women, which is respect for their peers, whatever their origin or activity within the home or society. And respect   is not only manners (smile, friendly behavior), but also attitudes toward women's options in society.

Chapter 6

Courtesy, Gender and Language

The following quote was in the document published by the United Nations Educational, Scientific and Cultural Organization (UNESCO) in 1999, under the title "Guidelines on Gender-Neutral Language":

"...A growing awareness that language does not merely reflect the way we think: it also shapes our thinking. If words and expressions that imply that women are inferior to men are constantly used, that assumption of inferiority tends to become part of our mindset. Hence, the need to adjust our language when our ideas evolve. Language is a powerful tool: poets and propagandists know this - as, indeed, do victims of discrimination".

Scholars of the language, especially those of feminist orientation have developed campaigns regarding the use of neutral language as a way to eradicate behaviors and attitudes that perpetuate discrimination against women and they originated the document cited above and should incorporate and propagate the use of neutral language in any society conscious of the need for change.

The use of masculine and feminine gender nouns have traditionally promoted sexist connotation attitudes which have been justified and also they have created certain myths about the condition of women in society. Many words have determined the identification of sex, regardless of the true sense and real meaning. For example, being polite is a masculine adjective in the Spanish language and that "linguistic determinant" has a general influence on women, especially Spanish-speaking ones. On the other hand, the use of feminine as equivalent of weakness allows certain advantages in society, which have been the main characteristic of the presence of women in society. In summary, much of the efforts of the social reformers to establish terms of gender equity in society are overshadowed by ancient and outdated prejudices based on the use of the language, which is one of the basic tools of human communication.

In the case of Spanish, like all romance languages, it is a gender-based language (male, female), therefore language activities originally assigned only to men and today exercised by both sexes, still have a clear male connotation and ignored women that practice them UNESCO recommended in order to achieve recognition of women in society that "...Gender equality does not mean that men and women are the same, but that their opportunities and life

27

chances are equal... It will be possible only when the language and thinking reflect a balanced and educated expression without exclusion of gender, ethnicity or culture."

Language as a reason for perpetuating discrimination not only in terms of gender, and it has been one of the topics that raise more questions among the so-called post-feminist current linguists.

In languages like Spanish for example, the use of adjectives have a different meaning when it is used for a man or a woman For example, we see the adjective "courteous" that by custom has been assigned to a man. In the case of women is easily associated with "courtesan", but already this term is commonly used for a female of easy behavior dishonest or kind of prostitute conduct of a woman. (Spanish words: cortés (man), cortesana (women)).

A very common case in Spanish is the term of public figure (hombre público), which refers to someone involved in affairs of the community. On the other hand if it is used "public woman"(mujer pública) this phrase refers to a prostitute. It's amazing but this differentiation of use of an adjective between men and women has a specific name accepted by scholars of Spanish language. The use of these adjectives has different semantic value and when applied to men or women have different connotations, which are called "apparent dual"(duales aparentes). And, this questionable practice reflects, once again, the paternalistic nature of the origins of language, especially Spanish.

Another example of manipulation of the language in Spanish is the word vanity (feminine noun), which usually is understood as a feminine characteristic assigned to women and alien to males. Its meaning is intrinsically - by custom - associated with women. On the other hand the term courteous is assigned to men and it is not associated with women. Thus, unconsciously most women have developed behavior where it is required that the man should be courteous, but not women. The adjective is very masculine to transfer it into a female meaning shows almost inappropriate behavior to find it and dispense it among women. And, in the case of vanity, where the man is usually considered not vain; but the woman is. Those concepts do not reflect reality because men or women are somewhat naturally vain.

The problem is not just Spanish. Other languages also have their restrictions. Dale Spander, an Australian feminist scholar of development of language in relation to gender, in her book "Man has Made the Language", considered the limitation of language as a real barrier to the equality and expression of reality. And, she believes the cause of this limitation is the patriarchal origins of the language. In this sense in everyday life we can see the consequences of these restrictions, specifically in the case of the treatment of women.

This prior patriarchal existence of the language, before feminist movements, definitely influences our behavior. For example, in the Spanish language there are not words to describe a form of fraternity among women. Interestingly the same word (hermandad) is applied both for men and women. And, automatically there is more identification of this word as a male action or to describe fraternities or religious or social groups. This situation has played an important role in the account of facts of human history, as it has been documented in detail the behavior between men but not of women.

It is appropriate to mention that in English there is a difference of the sense of fraternity, friendship among men, (brotherhood) and among women (sisterhood). This reflects a breakthrough in terms of relations between women from English-speaking background, because they do have a word that describe a better understanding of what solidarity among women means.

Therefore a word close to these concepts in Spanish would be solidarity (mutual support), which has a universal connotation, and it can be identified as a feminine adjective. Unfortunately, women do not internalize the concept, or practice regularly solidarity acts with other women. Thus, by practice (not being fraternal between women), instead of the language serving as a communication channel it becomes a barrier isolating the individuals, not only women but also men.

Another aspect of the limitations of communication and language is the fact that while acknowledging that women use more polite and courteous terms, it is also true that they practice them mostly when there are men in their presence. Many times on the pretext of creating agreement between females themselves, they use a disrespectful vocabulary that ultimately affects the harmonious relationship between members of the same gender. On the other hand, as experts in England recently said, younger generations currently consider the use of the appropriate language as a sign of submission that has been outdated by new generations. Hence the fashion of using improper words and profanity not only among men but also among women aggravates the existing situation between females.

In general the language limits women because of its patriarchal origins and it becomes a barrier to exercise a better approach between females. It may be added that in recent years new generations of women are more aggressive in their expressions as a way to compensate their inability to communicate due to natural limitations of language outlined in its origins. On the other hand, with currents behaviors (under the auspices of the media) regarding excessive competition as the only way to achieve success; women are in conflict between themselves more than ever. For this reason it is important to change the use of language as a discriminatory element between women themselves. There are changes and they should keep increasing. Today for example, it is more often to use terms like congressperson, firefighter, and police officer, instead of always attaching the word man at the end of the word.

Between Women, Friends or Enemies?

It is important to remember that not only the meaning of a word is used to exclude females themselves; but also the way the word is expressed. For example, it happens between women from different social-economic levels where a distant and contemptuous treatment is used as a very common form of aggression. Women use language to establish differences between themselves, if they are not from the same group. This fact reflects the persistence of similar attitudes, which frequently occur between the man and the woman (dominant-dominated). In other words, the members of the female sex use this type of language as one of their main weapons, repeating the same patterns of behavior of men, and they are not always the most constructive ones.

The Spanish Royal Academy of Language (RAE), has recently issued a report questioning the presence of publications under the auspices of feminists, which give guidelines for better use of language in favor of the elimination of discrimination, and thus promotes a real visibility of women in society as well as to prevent gender-based violence. This new position of the RAE belies any statement made by their representatives in the past. Curiously, in previous years RAE acknowledged being in coordination with a group of feminists in order to make propositions that would be mostly accepted without promoting "feminist activism". Also, the Director of the RAE, Garcia de la Concha, during an International Meeting of Spanish Language, held in 2007, explained that gender is a grammatical meaning word. "Now, it is politically correct to put male and female when someone addresses the public - referring to the insistence of many feminists asking to include both genders in all text-, when traditional regulations indicate that in such cases "the male is enough". "We must respect the laws of the language which are a product of the economy", said Garcia de la Concha. "If not, they start doubling, when there are terms of common reference ", concluded the academician. Garcia de la Concha in a very unclear attitude explained, "The RAE doesn't want to be a feminist or sexist, but be at a happy medium point ". It is something really incomprehensible, because the language deficiencies ignore and seriously are affecting the recognition of the presence and progress of woman in society. Currently of the 46 members of the RAE, five are women who were chosen by the other 41 members. This is a vicious circle that delays a necessary and just recognition of the presence of women in all levels of society. The RAE is not current with the present times, and it is not correcting attitudes of past centuries. The problem is aggravated by the extent of this negligence, especially in the mass media where it is more evident the disadvantage of woman when we see her portrayed and treated as an object.

In summary we can say the use of patriarchal language (especially in Spanish) has not been changed for the better, which hinders equal treatment of women. As a result of this usage, women are not practicing forms of more harmonious and equal language between themselves. Every effort to overcome this limitation will only be effective if women practice a proper language in every day life with our fellow human beings. Making use of language that includes and does not exclude the presence of women is a challenge to be overcome by the same women. See Annex A (Examples from Guideline on Gender –Neutral Language)

Chapter 7

Treatment Between Women

What woman has not experienced the different attitudes of a female receptionist when she talks to a man, and when she talks to a woman? In some cases she makes an effort to be non-discriminatory, but in general the treatment is different. The behavior of centuries prevails: women have to be more gentle with men, but not with women.

Some years ago, my husband and I flew to South America and we were using a Central American airline company. The flight included several stops and the trip lasted more than fifteen hours. There was a moment when a female passenger felt sick and asked for a hot drink to a member of the flight staff, who was a woman. The flight attendant ignored the female passenger despite the fact that she insisted several times. When my husband saw how the lady was ignored, he stood up and requested a cup of coffee as if it was for him, to the same crewmember. Unbelievably, she brought him coffee in less than five minutes. She was surprised when he gave the drink to the lady who had been asking for it to the same flight attendant. The incident was real and variations of the same are common in different circumstances of our lives.

Many times women have suffered in one-way or another from this mistreatment of woman to woman. And, probably the toughest experiences of discrimination have come from women themselves. This type of behavior is given with greater intensity in societies where women have a distinct situation of disadvantage and domination.

If one takes a quick look at the hundreds of manuals of behavior, it is difficult to find one where it addresses the conduct between women, either in public or private situations. And, it needs to be reiterated that if respect is not practiced between women then discrimination will continue in society.

In this regard it is advisable for women to remember: (at offices and public places)

• When a female customer demands attention, she deserves the same level of respect as is given to a man.

• Every person deserves to be treated friendly and professionally regardless of his or her gender.

• The required information should be answer clearly, and avoid attitudes and discriminatory comments. Many times a female receptionist or office worker, abuses or mistreats a female client with gestures and the way she looks to the woman requesting information or attention.

• In the case of a female customer with physical or mental limitations, do not ignore her with the excuse that she requires the attention of a male. It is important to note that the first approach and attention given reflects the true meaning of mutual human support.

• Body language can create an unwanted situation. It is advisable to avoid ignoring the other person or not looking at her when she explains her problem or question. That attitude reflects a lack of education and humanism. Or, when a receptionist or a clerk looks at her female customer with doubt or question about what she said, without any basis. This kind of conduct shows a lack of respect for members of the same sex.

Chapter 8

Women in the Work Place

" I've been sabotaged so many times on the job by another woman that I finally left the corporate world and started my own business ", said Roxy Westpahl, in an article published by the New York Times (2007). She currently has her company in Arizona and still remembers when 30 years ago other woman abused her verbally during a job interview that left her sobbing. I had a similar experience more than two decades ago, when a woman hierarchical superior at my job in Lima, Peru, justified her opposition to my promotion during a personal interview. As she stated " I was not like her who was descended from a military elite, which allowed her to study in Europe". After such a painful and disappointing interview, my life changed, and I'm not going to deny it. I decided to pursue different goals and career and I believe it was for the best. What I cannot forget is that another woman was the cruelest opponent to recognize my professional capacity.

Studies in the United States (Berkeley, California) and Canada University of Waterloo) in 2007 indicated that women continue to be abusive with their female partners at work. The growing presence of women in the work force in modern society has created unforeseen situations because they reflect the ancient and negative attitude between females. This finding reminds me of another experience I had almost three decades ago when I entered the office assigned to me as a Diplomat Officer at the Foreign Affairs Ministry in Peru. The first reaction of the secretaries was disappointment because I was not a man. And, they did not hesitate to let me know about it. Then I tried to develop a relationship with them which was unconventional, for example talking to them about their issues and participating in their events in order to gain their trust and support. I am sure I was never looked at in the same way as a male from the point of view of a professional and hierarchically superior. Things have apparently changed, but still there are behaviors that reaffirm the discrimination between women. We must not forget that it occurs in different directions. For example, there are cases where female professionals feel superior to other women colleagues because they have a title or higher position at the office. Or, the secretary who in some cases for sexual favors has more power in the office than any other professional; these circumstances shape behavior between women,

Between Women, Friends or Enemies?

especially when they come to power.

The abuse between women in the work place apparently shocked the women's movement in its own foundations. Peggy Klaus, Executive of a Berkeley company, has called this phenomenon: "the Pink Elephant" at the work place. The author wonders how woman can ascend if she mistreats her colleagues of the same sex anywhere at the workspace? (New York Times, 2009).

Susan Shapiro Barah in her book, "Tripping the Queen of the Promotion, the Truth About the Rivalry Between Women"(2009), indicates that women are more concerned with competing against their same gender co-workers than with their male counterparts."

In this regard it is important to mention another aspect of the same scenario: the role of the assistants, and the countless times were the assistant takes more power than she should tor their females co-workers who for various reasons assistants assume a dictatorial attitude. Thus, we see how many of these female assistants decide who sees or doesn't see their supervisor. In these circumstances, women are the less fortunate; unless you have a relationship of friendship or interest with the assistant. In other words, female administrative assistants many times are harder with their same gender co-workers.

Those attitudes, even though in some cases they are disguised, to a greater or lesser extent are still common in the work

40

place. The same article from the New York Times, mentioned above, includes how American and Canadian researchers agree about the pursuit of a common goal among females may avoid these unpleasant confrontations. "We believe that the sense of self-worth of women when they pursue a common objective, this helps them to be mutually supportive...." "To have that satisfaction, women need to be aware of sharing their identity as women," says Grace Lau of the Canadian University of Waterloo.

It is the truth that a solidary attitude is a basic requirement and the most important issue is what women feel internally. Females must learn to know themselves and appreciate their unique qualities. Once they develop their self-esteem then it may be possible for them to accept the qualities of other woman and thus they will be more productive as a team.

In order to promote women's equality and respect in the work place the following suggestion are helpful for administrative assistants.

• To be affable and informative with the public and co-workers without distinction of gender. The use of appropriate and inclusive (neutral) language needs to be the main feature of her communication.

• To search for solutions not conflicts in her environment.

• To avoid confrontation among co- workers, especially between women. Unite not divide.

- Be sure to eradicate gossip and murmurings.

- It is important to value and respect the qualities of their female co-workers at the hierarchical level. Everybody deserves the same respect. To be aware of her gender and role to help to change attitudes to create harmony between people.

- It is essential to accept and respect her female supervisor, the same as a man.

Chapter 9

Women in the Management Field

According to statistics given by the latest published United States Census (2009), in the United States 50 percent of executive women have management positions. Also, it shows that females are only part of the 15.7 per cent of the CEOs of the Fortune 500 corporations, and 15.2 per cent of management positions within this elite group of powerful companies.

Now, we observe more frequently how women, by different circumstances, have achieved a position of power in various instances of public and private life. Unfortunately, the fact is that if some of them are aware of their role as agents for change in society, others are not. The problem also lies in the acceptance of women as a team leader. According to recent reports of the Gallup pull in all the United States, out of women over the age of 50, 39% prefer a male boss, and 27% prefer women. In general, today 56% of women of all ages prefer men as a head of an office against 30% who support women in the same position.

These figures are not so encouraging if we take in account the increase of women in the labor force in the last 30 years. There is no doubt there are more women in the work place and therefore their numbers are growing in executive or management positions. For this reason, it is good to remember the following:

• Women in modern society have more of the same opportunities as men. If a woman is aware of her role as an agent for change, when she acts as a supervisor, she must demonstrate equal respect and support to her female and male co-workers.

• When a female boss addresses her colleagues, she should maintain a neutral attitude. Unfortunately, it is commonly observed women in power still feel diminished in front of men. On the other hand, in front of women they are excessive in the exercise of their authority.

• Women need to facilitate the development of a colleague for her/his ability without favoritism. Females tend to make the same mistakes as men in power, which contributes to the perpetuation of patterns of behavior that keep inequality in society. In this sense, it is important to avoid the other extreme. For example, in a well known chain of Italian restaurants in the United States, one of the main executives is a female and she has established rules of overprotection and promotion of women, creating unrest and antipathy of males co-workers towards their female ones. It is important to avoid contributing to the myth that the female supervisor is synonymous with confliction and bitterness. The lack of experience and tradition of females in power often makes them, (once they reach an executive position) inaccessible and petulant individuals. These attitudes do not contribute to an atmosphere of equality and solidarity in society. A recommended behavior is to maintain communication with the co-workers (males or females), accept suggestions, avoid personal comments and above all, look to female colleagues with respect and equality.

The abusive, discriminatory, and illegal treatment that many men developed to exercise their power in the past should not recur when a woman has a similar position. If it does occur, then there is no change at all, and "only pants have been changed by skirts", and still there is no human advancement in society.

There are, on the other hand, many cases when women use questionable ways to ascend to power. There are still circumstances where due to non-professional reasons and for personal favoritism many females have access to positions of importance. In this sense a woman herself with greater awareness and more confidence in controlling her life and respect for her rights can contribute to the eradication of these patterns of behavior which cause the increase of female segregation.

When women continue with traditional models it is because

society itself has not evolved and it is up to the same women to eliminate this situation. It is not only a matter of quotas or laws. It is the responsibility of every woman to respect and be respected, only then she can establish the difference and be on the right path to construct an equitable society.

Chapter 10

Is There an Abuse of Sexual Harassment?

Laws are important, but depend on to whom are they applied, because in many cases the human mind and society have misrepresented the initial objective of these rules especially in terms of respect and equality of people at the work place. A constant attitude of manipulating legality and forgetting moral principles is what prevails in the majority of cases of sexual harassment. This behavior shows, once more, the lack of respect that women have for themselves and to other females in general.

There are many allegations of sexual harassment where usually a woman accuses a man of compromising her moral standards. Some of those accusations are true; others are not. It is also relevant mention the case of women who abuse their power of sexual attraction in order to get favors from men.

Between Women, Friends or Enemies?

In addition, in the case of sexual harassment of men to women it is good to note the peculiar thing about these cases when any times they were denounced the plaintiff has failed to achieve her purpose of advancing professionally, based on favors to and from the offender. Of course not all cases are the same and there are abuses of power from supervisors to subordinates.

The woman who wants to move forward on her own, usually is in solidarity with her gender, is respectful of the rights of her colleagues without discrimination of sex; she also avoids playing with the traditional elements commonly used by man to perpetuate himself in power.

A case worth mentioning is the one given during the process of the confirmation of Judge Clarence Thomas to the United States Supreme Court in 1991. At that time a former associate of the jurist; attorney Anita Hill, claimed to have been subjected to sexual harassment on the part of the proposed judge when they worked together in the years before. In front of millions of viewers the African-American attorney detailed verbal excesses that Thomas had with her. Strange enough, she followed him to a second job. The question everybody had in mind was why she did not denounce the case at the time and waited so long to bring to light her accusations. In the end, the complaint did not affect the appointment of Judge Thomas who was confirmed by the United States Congress. Other colleagues who coincide in offices where Dr. Thomas and Dr. Hill were working did not support statements made by Dr. Hill in this case. Political analysts considered the case as a maneuver to avoid the appointment of another conservative member to the U.S. Supreme Court. On the other hand, some feminists considered that it was a mistake not to take into account the declarations of Anita Hill; but other women's rights advocates thought that the situation showed very common cases of sexual harassment. According to people following the case, different circumstances should be taken into consideration; for example when the alleged victim has expectations of benefits from the aggressor, she is passive. Also, it could be that she, due to the aggressor's power either political or economic is afraid to denounce the fact. However, according to the same observers, when the victim feels that there is no possibility of "gain", she reports the case as a very subtle form of blackmail or revenge.

In the case of Anita Hill, the odd fact is that after nearly 20 years after the event, "out of the blue", Judge Thomas's wife reopened the controversy requesting publicly that Dr. Anita Hill apologize to her husband. Dr. Hill has flatly refused.

Regarding the same case, recently it has emerged that a third woman, Lillian McEween, a lawyer, who is retired and had an extensive experience in American public service claimed she had been the mistress of Judge Thomas for many years. Also, now she agrees with Dr. Hill about the morbid and disrespectful behavior of the Supreme Court Judge. She also has given other details that corroborate the lack of fitness of Judge Thomas for the position where he is now. The question is, why did Dr. McEween not come forward before in order to unmask this individual? Why did she not support Dr. Hill? She has replied that she came forward but she was not taken into account. Apparently the problem was the rivalry and lack of respect between those two women. In the end, the country has suffered the consequences. It is pertinent to mention that legal observers have expressed concerns, because during the past years as a Supreme Court Judge, Thomas has proved to be very personal in his judgments and they do not reflect legal expertise from a jurist of high academic training. His vote has made it possible that social rights won by the people in the past, are now in retreat.

This case of grave consequences for the American people could have been avoided if Dr. Hill and Dr. McEween made public what they knew about aspects of the non-public side of Thomas' life, which could be considered objectionable and of great importance for his performance as a Supreme Court Judge. That action could be possible if those two women had more solidarity between them. And, if they come forward it would show that they really had a greater social conscience.

It is pertinent to recognize there are also cases of women who think that equality means to mimic wrongdoing of men, especially in cases of sexual harassment where women harass men. Abuse of power is not exclusive to the male. Such circumstances respond to the lack of social awareness of women in today's society that is undermining any qualitative step of the women in building a better world.

Chapter 11

Fashion and Women

Fashion has been considered a constant companion of every woman. Even though there are extreme cases, actually women have always developed a very close relationship between clothing and her self-esteem. It feels good to dress appropriately and not to clash with our surroundings. We cannot ignore that those practices, are also important requirements for developing socially and professionally. Of course, trying always to dress with out exaggeration. In addition, the interest for fashion is no stranger to men. Both men and women, have the same penchant to enjoy wearing a fashionable wardrobe and feel good. Thus, you cannot assign this practice as a unique characteristic of women. Actually, fashion has as sound social implications, because when it is exaggerated it disrupts the harmony between members of the same gender, and also the environment in which a group develops exhibiting the importance of how fashion is utilized.

Additionally, if it is recognized that fashion apparel is part of human behavior, then it is also good to remember that "gurus" of fashion are not so alien to social movements. Their styles, often underestimated by social experts, have reflected the development and integration of women in society.

Through a brief and recent historical view, we can see that after the Second World War, there has been growing presence of women in various fields of work in society. French fashion designers recognized this change and incorporated them in their new creations . Particularly Coco Chanel, who with the famous skirt and jacket set (female response to the male suit) revolutionized and facilitated the presence of women in the labor force. Previously she already had introduced pants in the daily feminine wardrobe. Thus, her contribution is important because with her style she expresses the changes of that current time; and also how female wardrobes were divided between social and working attire, which has been the main characteristic in the past 60 years. However, times are now changing.

In the beginning of the 21st century, women's ways of dressing were modified. Under the pretext of the self-assurance the female body started to be exhibited to a greater extent. The division between social and working clothing has been blurred and, again, dictators of fashion are not alien to the true meaning of this questionable trend. Especially in moments when fashion points to an image of childish female styles with kind of "baby dolls"(intimate) clothing. This type of today's fashion ridicules most women and makes them go back in history to an anecdotal presence, which goes against a real and constant role of women in society, especially at the work place. Also the trend towards a "Drag Queen" (she males) style has spread everywhere. Shoes that look like stilts, exaggerated styles of dresses and makeup, which denotes a confusion of identification, can have serious consequences to female behavior. These trends can be seen as a breakthrough of groups seeking to blur the identity of the traditional genders.

Within this trend of exaggeration of styles we have seen young women and others not so young, exposing large cleavage or wearing tight pants showing much of their bodies at the office. A very daring way of dressing that recalls the great cleavage of the courts of Louis XIV, coincidence? No. This fashion is reinforcing the idea of women as a decoration or object, not as a human being.

Women today have been over-sexualized by the media. And, one of the consequences is how females are giving an excessive and growing importance to their outside appearance that goes beyond clothing and the quest for beauty. In this effort women are losing their essence. Today it is not only how to dress or use makeup but also they are looking for permanent change through surgical procedures. This situation leads us to reflect how women are losing themselves in trivial matters and have forgotten their role as an agent for change. Women as sex objects, with some variations, have become stronger in today's society, perpetuating roles carried from past centuries. Rivalry, competition, and conflict based on their external appearance are the main issues. More attractive physically and less questionable intellectually women are more accepted. That is the golden rule we often see today, and in essence, women have moved backwards.

Returning to how to dress, there is no doubt that wardrobe helps people to look better; however it is a double-edged sword, which allows a person to be taken seriously or just to represent decorative roles. And do not forget, between women any excess can make them uncomfortable.

Therefore, it is important to be aware of what women are looking to portray with clothes. Style can be a reason to look better, but it is not the total answer to feel better. The inner part, spiritual development, self-esteem, and morality cannot be ignored because it can be seen in the image we project. The way women dress is a form of self-expression and it creates bridges of approach or rejection in the work place.

It will be advisable to remember that when women decide what to wear, especially at work, to take in consideration the following: Low necklines invite to distract the person we are talking to, and thus the message that she wants to communicate is not taken seriously.

- Comfortable clothes help that a person can look more professional.

- Stilettos or heels, and platform shoes, which cause women to be more concerned with looking sexy, don't look professional. It is not suitable for everyday use in the work place.

- To dress with the latest fashion, or use expensive brands, is not synonymous or guarantees of elegance and distinction.

- Quality and good taste are skills learned with observation and reflect the real self-esteem of the person.

- Work places are not catwalks. A discrete, elegant wardrobe replaces the most complete wardrobes from all over the world.

- When finding out about the event you are invited to or going to assist it is advisable to wear the appropriate attire in order to avoid unwanted situations.

- Spread among young women certain basic principles of good taste in clothing and discretion.

It is vital to remember that the outside appearance is important, but not the only requirement to be accepted or taken seriously. Also, wardrobe should not be restricted as the irreplaceable element to recognize the professional capacity among a circle of friends or co-workers. It will be good to remember that wearing inappropriate attire can make members of the same sex uncomfortable and subjected to situations that are against their moral principles. More exposed for example, creates confusion or surprise for those who are not used to exposing her body. The way a person dresses can make the difference

Gladys Morales-Smith

how people behave towards them regardless of their sex.

Chapter 12

Education

At all times, education is a crucial support in the progress of all social groups. Within this context, undoubtedly women have had a discriminatory treatment that many times has been perpetuated by other females.

Women as Teachers

From the first years of training in many cases, their female teachers expose many girls to exclusion. This can create irreversible damage. Discrimination of sex or ethnicity in the social world starts and marks the life of a person since the early years of instruction, especially in mixed schools where girls undergo a subtle aggression that generates a major bewilderment in new generations of women. In the classroom, for example, many times females are marginalized in terms of access to knowledge. Girls, usually, do not receive instruction with the same dedication offered to a male student or, sometimes a girl or boy with a lighter skin.

With great concern, it can be observed that in large cities where the multiplicity of ethnic groups and cultures are reflected in schools, one of the major causes of student drop out rates among girls is the tactless treatment and lack of support from their female teachers. Traditional statistics refer only to external elements like socioeconomic status, family dysfunction and gender. These numbers do not recognize causes where many children are victims of unscrupulous teachers (male or female) who submit them to situations of isolation, humiliation and rejection. Girls suffer more intensely from this type of harassment, which exists at all socioeconomic levels and in all parts of the world. Specifically with the high rates of migration from the South to the North, children and young people who are subjected to greater discrimination are the children of those immigrants, turning them into pariahs and outcasts.

What to do?

Some suggestions that female teachers can implement include:

• Treat all students equally without sex discrimination. The use of non-sexist language promotes self-esteem and integration between young people regardless of their sex.

Between Women, Friends or Enemies?

• Exist in today society a much-needed special effort to reaffirm the self-worth of its members, whether these are women or men.

• Protection and support from teachers (male or female), communicated to students naturally and effectively, make a difference and those guides of behavior are a source of inspiration for young people (of both sexes). In addition, a positive role of educators will have a multiplier effect, which will shape the conduct of generations where gender will not be a reason for exclusion.

• Treat female or male students equally.

Parents should communicate with their children (daughters and sons),and maintain a constant contact with teachers. Only a close communication allows them to know if these young people are subjected to harassment or other forms of discrimination. Very often parents believe that sending children to school is enough. Unfortunately, the "school adventure" that starts from the pre-school level is very delicate for girls and boys. Many teachers take their frustrations and resentments to their classrooms and those problems are reflected in their treatment to emotionally weaker minors.

The present awkward situation requires a conscious assessment from the educational system, regarding a better psychological evaluation of teachers and assistants to determine if a person can perform professionally her/his role as a guide for the new generations.

Gladys Morales-Smith

A common aspect today all over the world is the acceleration of migratory movements, which has caused many children and their parents to move to cities or towns outside their place of origin. Because of the deficiency to communicate in the new environment and many times with a different language, children are victims of discrimination that makes their educational integration harder. In this sense, there are cases of a person who takes advantage of their bilingual status and, without sufficient training is in charge of the sensitive education of these children. To disguise their limitations those unprepared instructors blame students of having a disability or limitations of learning. For example, those instructors advise hiring speech therapists to treat children when their only problem is not being able to speak the local language. But "these experts" demands come from so-called educators who are unaware of teaching methods and stigmatize the child with non-existent disabilities to justify their inability and ignorance. For this reason, it is important to monitor education of immigrants anywhere in the world. People without training who speak the language of origin of the students do not guarantee suitability or fair treatment to the learners. And it is good to remember women usually are the majority of the teaching staff and have a leading role.

It is also appropriate to mention another growing problem, which is, sexual harassment in the classroom. This behavior occurs more between teacher (male) and pupil (girl or boy). Although, it is important to mention that lately there has been public cases where female teachers harassed girls or boys. In general, those cases show the crisis of moral values not only in schools but also in all society. Therefore it requires constant evaluation from the authorities to prevent abuses of children' innocence and integrity.

At all times, it is advisable that constant communication between parents and their children and remind them that nobody has the right to touch the inappropriate parts of their body. Particularly if it is a teacher (male or female) offering favors in exchange for accepting situations against moral principles. Again, without distinction of sex, parents should put emphasis on education and prevention of their loss of their children' integrity. It is always good to promote communication among boys and girls with their friends and parents and mates, which will guarantee, to some extent, the control of any abuse.

Although the aim of this book is to establish guidelines for better treatment between women, we cannot ignore the fact that all of us live in a community where both men and women are subject to discrimination which marks their exclusion in society. It is important to emphasize the role of female teachers with female learners because this is the sector of students that traditionally had received greater aggression, discrimination, and postponement. And, take in consideration that a common discrimination with girls often happens with regard to math and science opportunities.

Chapter 13

Women and Mothers

There is not doubt that motherhood is a blessing from nature to women. But, are all women ready for this mission? Are they honestly ready to assume their maternity? Are women in solidarity with their daughters? The ambivalence of feelings of love and hatred as one of the characteristics of motherhood is another aspect to consider. Real life shows how many mothers find themselves with conflicting feelings not complying with traditional concepts of motherhood. And it is a fact that throughout the world many teen-agers are having children and they are not prepared to be mothers, which makes the theme more serious and complex.

The positive side...

"I was a child so loved by my mother, and my older sister Dulce, so I cannot ask for more: I believe women love me and I love them in return". Françoise Giroud, "Arthur ou le Bonheur de Vivre/

Arthur or the happiness of Being", 1997. When we remember the expressions of the French writer Françoise Giroud, it is undoubtedly the multiplier effect of motherhood. It is clear how women as mothers in the majority of cases, make all the difference in the behavior of an individual's life, either women or men.

The downside...

Some decades ago, as a journalist, I had the opportunity to offer lectures to mothers of slum areas in Lima, Peru. Women complained about the misbehavior of their sons and daughters. About boys, they said they imitated their fathers and often received mistreatment not only from their husbands, but also from their sons. Some women did not talk too much about their daughters. The daughters were almost invisible, and the mothers always questioned the lack of respect from them. The vast majority of these women expected their daughters would find a husband as they got older, and then they would be protected. Mothers did not dispute the origin of the lack of self-respect or respect from their daughters, and always a tinge of rivalry characterized the relationship between them. And, this example can be applied to many countries where women are not so educated and not taught to value themselves.

These mothers defined the fate of their sons with an attitude of acceptance to the male power. Regarding their daughters, there was not an interest to teach them self-respect, or search for better horizons, concepts that were ignored by these mothers themselves. Daughters just repeat their mothers' own stories.

Another aspect in general is rivalry between mothers and daughters, and can also be found in the case described by Rita Adria in her journal which resulted in the film "The Sicilian girl" (2009). Rita was a young woman who, in revenge for the deaths of her father and brother, denounces the mafia in her village in the South of Italy. Her mother rejected Rita because she betrayed the mafia, and reminded Rita that she never wanted to have a baby when she learned she was waiting for her. Later in the film the mafia kills Rita. Then, the film shows how the mother destroys the tomb of her daughter. All facts were based on real events.

Similar cases are discussed in the book published recently by Barbara Almond entitled: "The Monster Inside, the Hidden Side of Motherhood". In the book Almond talks about mixed feelings of love and hate experienced by many mothers, also the shame, guilt and anxiety that those feelings engendered in them.

Of course, there is another side of the story, like the case of Madame Giroud where her closest female relatives helped her to love her gender. But in other cases, when there is rivalry between mother and daughter in their relations, the main characteristic is the inability to communicate mutual self-respect for them. Many mothers, not all, see their daughters as potential rivals, either because they are younger and look better or because the father shows special

65

attention to the female child. Feminists of her country because of her lack of radicalism challenged Madame Giraud, who became the first Minister of Women Affairs in France in the 1970's. Aside from this aspect of her governance, her life's achievements, undoubtedly are worthy of spreading. As she said in her book, her mother filled the absence left by her father who, since she was born made her feel guilty for not being born male. Curiously enough, the paternal treatment affected all her personal and professional life. In her memoirs, Madame Giroud described her feelings of guilt when she had to assume her post as Minister because she acted as her male counterparts, a fact that she considered a betrayal to the feminist movement. Regardless of these considerations, her success and sureness undoubtedly had a direct relationship with the treatment she received from her mother and her older sister.

There are other stories like the one of Isadora Duncan, the Californian artist who is an icon in terms of her avant-garde way of life; not only in dance but also in her behavior as a feminist in every sense of the word. In her book "My Life", she recounts that at age 12, when her parents divorced, she decided to defend the rights of women. Also, she recalled witnessing the fate of her mother and female friends being humiliated physically and spiritually by their spouses, who made her promise "never to lower herself in that degrading state (marriage)". So in this case another effect of relations between mother and daughter is noticed so that without words or gestures, a daughter receives from her mother's life a message to

avoid degrading situations to her human condition.

In May 2009, when Dr. Sonia Sotomayor accepted her nomination as a member of the Supreme Court of the United States, she expressed her appreciation and admiration to her mother saying, "thanks to her I am what I am and I am not even half of the woman she is." Her mother is a retired nurse who after the death of her husband raised and educated two young children. Her daughter is now the first woman of Hispanic origin who holds the highest rank in the United States Judicial System and Dr. Sotomayor's brother is a prominent physician.

The link between mother and daughter is a determining factor in the future behavior of that woman who will repeat or will cut the circle of discrimination and passivity in the society. The mother's influence is similar with male children.

Unfortunately, at the beginning of the 21st century, it is common to see everywhere, with some beautiful exceptions, (like the cases described above); it is perceived that still there is a perpetuation of questionable female patterns due to a new form of lack of recognition in society. Nevertheless, there are cases where the mother, instead of being a friend, confidant and adviser becomes mostly an instigator of conflict with conditions and demands that only provoke distant relationships where the daughter has no self-respect or respect for her mother or other members of her gender.

Between Women, Friends or Enemies?

Other mothers encourage questionable attitudes to their daughters. They use the excuse: "don't to be silly and repeat the naivety of their mother". In this manner, professional and educated women "train" their daughters to get what they want, no matter what and according to traditional molds, which are questionable in terms of "using their feminine attributes". It is not because of ignorant women who don't know how to educate their offspring, but well educated females who have no scruples to coach a new type of female, extremely self-absorbed and ambitious where solidarity and respect are principles that become void in their way of life. The proliferation of this type of women in society at every level contributes to the crisis of values in present society, which intensifies an unequal society.

And that is the kind of woman we see more today. But, is it what we really want for the good of society? I do not think so. The multiplier effect of mothers in society is undeniable. Despite today's modernisms a mother defines the behavior of the individual since the first years of life. Children of a prejudiced and unscrupulous mother will take in the fruits of those attitudes towards life. Many times we find young people (without distinction of sex) , being disrespectful, racists, bigots and; when we look into them, we find their parents are the origin of this mediocre attitude towards life.

In this new century, a real concern is to find how common young people are violent and without knowledge of being a real human being with morals and standards of life in a civilized society. For many, this kind of behavior among young people is a result of an irresponsible public education and their dysfunctional families. And, mothers, of course, have a decisive role.

What is advisable to do?

Taking into consideration the proximity and effect of the relationship between mother and child, it is good to remember that:

• Mothers should see their daughters (and sons) as their own mirror where the good experiences of growing up and personal fulfillment are multiplied. Most women encourage machismo between boys and girls since their birth, especially when they maintain overprotective attitudes. Daughters continue the chains of submission and low self-esteem learned since childhood through their mothers.

• Constructive criticism between mother and daughter, with tips and solutions must be taught in a logical and timely manner.

• Ethical values are very important and should be cultivated between parents and children. Some time ago a television show presented a young girl, who wanted to sell her virginity on Internet, she explained that the money obtained from the questionable transaction could help her family and she could also complete her education. The disrespectful way she treated her mother (the father was dead) belied her alleged good intentions. Her moral framework was completely confused, which was confirmed when it was proved that she was not a virgin and based on a non-sense technicality she insisted she was. A faint-heart mother went to a television judge to ask her daughter to reflect about this act of prostitution. The question is what kind of moral framework did this mother have when she educated her daughter? It is a question with many answers. On the other hand, there are other cases where mothers openly promote the prostitution of their daughters. In countries from Eastern Europe, for example (and is not the only case), where the trade in sex slaves is an epidemic, many mothers practically force their daughters into prostitution as in other poor countries around the world where poverty is confused with human misery.

It is important to remember:

1. The first five years in the education of an individual are decisive. The child accepts love and definition of values naturally.

2. People will be better prepared and more aware of their role and contribution to society for good and not for evil if a permanent presence of the parents is maintained. Despite the demands of contemporary life, along with a constant evaluation of the relationship between parents and children should be maintained.

3. Segregation, prejudice and social climbing are concepts initiated at home and usually the authorship belongs to a woman. Unfortunately, the experience of life makes us recognize the negative contribution of some women in the education of the new generations. Do not mistake constant physical presence, which can be

compensated by a good education with defined values that should be instilled from the first years of life. Thus, women should be aware of their important role in the formation of the individual's values.

Chapter 14

Relationships Between Female Relatives

It's sad to confirm that the validity of old patterns still exists in the relationships of female relatives. There we can find how the rivalry between sisters, sisters-in-law, mothers-in-law, and daughters-in-law remains with new features but in essence their behavior continue dividing the family. Sometimes playfully others seriously, there are always sarcastic comments to justify a confrontation between female relatives that is without basis. Many times it happens without not even knowing the other person, - for example, in the case of in-laws-, when a female relative speaks or acts against another before she even knows her in person. Many women approach their female in laws with prejudice and distrust.

Where does this behavior come from? History, has been mostly written by males, and has documented this "confrontation" in the relations of family members of the female gender. On the other hand, there are few times that we hear about stories where sisters or females-in-law are friends and live together harmoniously for the welfare of the family. Those cases do exist and have existed, but they have not been documented.

In the case of the relationship between sisters is something that is little documented. In essence, when there are problems of competitiveness and care, which start in childhood, and it is because there has been little attention in the affective development of the girls. That seed from childhood has terrible consequences because it generates a spiritual distance between them and thus conflicting relations are developed. It is the parents' duty to teach love and respect between sisters. They should avoid preferences and create strong feelings of solidarity between them. Nothing is more beautiful than the solid relationship of friendship and affection between sisters, it is a treasure that makes one see life with positivism and certainty. Respect for individuality is the main ingredient for successful relations between sisters.

When we interact with our female relatives, especially those originated by marriage, it requires great attention and finesse. Everybody has qualities and defects, recognition and respectfulness to them creates a fertile ground for the cultivation of a friendship that will strengthen the ties of each one of the family members.

Intrigue, jealousy, and envy among relatives begin with one of the family members, mostly women. With our individual effort history can be rewritten and create new bridges and forms of relationships that in the end will create a better world.

Jealousy for the mother-in-law, sister-in-law or females related by marriage is negative. It is important to recognize the problem, which occurs in all socioeconomic levels to a greater or lesser extent and it is important to find solutions. Healthy, honest and sincere approaches will open doors for a vigorous and harmonious relationship where the whole family will be benefited.

It would be good to remember:

• A sister is connected by a bond of blood, of education, of common dreams and, it is good to respect and expect respect from her. Competition is out of place and loyalty is an inseparable ingredient in the love and the relationship between sisters.

• Before speaking badly or against a mother-in-law, sister or any in-laws it is necessary to know them and, if there is no affinity set a ground of respect without animosity or prejudice. Avoid isolation. Friendly relationships without conflict are ideal.

• Recognize that before knowing a partner, she/he has a family with parents and siblings and they have to be respected as a whole family.

• Be aware that no one can force affection, but it is advisable to promote a relationship where constructive and healthy feelings should be put into practice. We should avoid the common prejudices against a sister-in-law because she is bad. Or because she is my mother in law, I must confront her. On the other hand it is advisable to remember that the "in-laws" should not interfere in the life of a couple.

- It is advisable to respect   sons and daughters alike as well as their partners (son or daughter in laws).

- No one can assume roles they do not deserve. A couple needs time and privacy; the presence of mothers-in-law, sisters-in-law, or another in-law relative should be limited and be careful not to ruin the couples' relationships.

- And, when it comes to sisters, mothers, cousins, or aunts, by blood or in laws, find common grounds based on a healthy and positive knowledge of them, and remember do not prejudge or comment without any reason. We all have the same fears, dreams and wishes, and to recognize them makes us strong and supportive.

CHAPTER 15

Female Friendship

In different countries and cultures female friendship reflects the reality of where they develop. Elaine Audet, the Canadian writer in her book "The Thinking Heart, Counterpoint of Friendship Between Women" explains this situation and stated "In Muslin countries for example, friendship is for females a survival weapon to overcome their cultural beliefs". Currently is the case in countries such as Algeria, Afghanistan, Iran and Bangladesh. In the same book the author refers to the absence of historical texts where a reference is made to the friendship between women. She adds, "Rare theorists who have treated the theme of friendship between women admit that it is a pleasure of life (of these women). The same source recognizes the difference between the limits of friendship and lesbianism, which is different because lesbianism is the choice of

76

some women to be related exclusively with women in some aspects of their life. In a friendship the issue of fusion matters more than a lucid recognition of the uniqueness of the other and his or her autonomy, which is not the case in the passion of love that is marked by the exclusivity and more or less a blind desire, according to Audet. Personally she thinks that friendship goes beyond any attempt of categorization, gender or otherwise, and friendship is simply born, paraphrasing the French author Montaigne, "because you are, then I am", described the Canadian author.

This ideal form of relationship between women, as we see it varies from country to country. In Spanish-speaking countries for example, female friendship reflects centuries of exclusion and today the effects are still perceived this way as to how women relate to each other. Between female friends relations are superficial and few instances have meaningful connotations. Individualism and competition mark a hallmark mostly inherited by the Spaniards. Between exclusively Native Americans (North, Central and South), there is a kind of gender solidarity, similar to the Arabs, but not in the individual and intimate way found in the case of the Europeans or Americans especially after the feminist movement. Although it is advisable to make note that rivalry and envy among women exists in all cultures, with rare exceptions.

In Latin American for instance there exists a lack of solidarity in terms of mutual respect between mestizo and Native Americans that manifests itself mostly in actions of discrimination, infidelity and betrayal. And, almost always the trophy is to obtain a man's preference. We can find this behavior in other countries, but they are less frequent. Low self-esteem is the main ingredient for this unfair conduct between women. In The United States there has been an evolution and today it is more common to find an increasing importance to consider pure, platonic friendship between women as an important ingredient in modern life. Dr. Ruthellen Josselson, co-author of "The Best Friends: the Pleasures and Dangers of the Friendship Between Girls and Women (Three Rivers Press, 1998) recognizes the importance of treasuring our friends and not putting them aside. As she said, "Every time we are very busy with work and family, the first thing we do is put aside our friends. That is really an error, because women are a source of strength between themselves. We take care of us. And we need to have a space without pressure where we can have a conversation as the one we have between women, it is a comforting experience..."

Recent studies at the University of California of Los Angeles reveals that the friendship between women has positive effects on their mental health, because it helps them to cope with stressful moments. Sharing and talking about their problems with friendly people, especially among women, according to this study enables the production of a hormone oxytocin, the same hormone that is in charge of the contractions of the uterus in childbirth and breast milk production and it causes feelings of affection between women. This experience allows them to cope with difficult situations that undermine their mental health and avoiding these situations increases the life expectancy of women. This same research has been made between men and women and reflects a new vision regarding a historical belief that, unlike men, women don't develop bonds of friendship between them.

Another proof of the study is the effect of women's' friendships on physical health is the investigation of Doctors, Candyce H. Kroenke, Laura D. Kubzansky, Eva S. Schernhammer, Michelle D. Holmes and Ichrio Kawachi at the Universities of Berkeley, School of Public Health from Harvard, and the Hospital of Women from the School of Medicine from Harvard School in Boston. Respectively, they came to the following conclusion: "after an investigation between 2,835 women diagnosed with cancer it was noted that isolated women had a high risk of mortality after having been diagnosed with the disease. Those who had greater survival rate indicated they had the support of friends and close relatives".

Although many times some women do not value the presence of a female friend who is always ready to listen and share experiences, this kind of behavior and feelings of solidarity between women exists and are part of their existence as proven and ratified by scientific research as mentioned before.

The "other side of the coin" shows also us that there is a shared secret, which influences women not to trust one another and explains that the abuse between women is a common practice; recent studies corroborate this affirmation. Kelly Valen, in 2010 published her book: "The Twisted Sisterhood. Unrevealing the Dark Legacy of Female Friendship ". Through her work she offered another view and confirms this statement. The author indicates that based on a survey among more than three thousand women from all United States, she has come to the conclusion that 84 percent of them said they have suffered terribly in the hands of other women. Also, 88 percent of these females felt hardness and negativity from other women, and 96 percent of the surveyed want something better in the treatment of women and girls.

These percentages are worrisome because it reaffirms the concept that women are still divided as always. The mass media does not help and, on the contrary, contributes to that "traditional" female confrontation.

But, what is female friendship like today?

Aside from theorists and hundreds of books written on the subject, there is a great truth: life is easier with good friends. Their support helps us to overcome moments of sadness, difficulties and also to celebrate moments of joy and triumph. A sincere friendship is a form of love, where materialistic interest and omission do not exist. Neither competition nor the curiosity for failures or other misfortune is part of real friendship. But, how many times do we find ourselves under situations where we feel disappointed by the inexplicable behavior of a female friend?

It is very true that often times women friends demand what they do not give and, instead of creating conditions for stable relationships they promote the development of superficial ties with fears and lack of communication. Traditionally relationships between women have been inaccurately portrayed. Either female friendship has been assigned an anecdotal, dramatic form, or it has become confused with lesbianism, or, on the other hand, its importance has been diminished intentionally.

We can perceive that main stream society has tried to undermine women's ability to establish valuable and spiritual relationships where the bond goes beyond any passing interest as commonly happens between men.

In addition to the superficiality, the relationship between women has been traditionally characterized with gossip and intrigue. On the contrary, every day more documents are being discovered where women express their feelings of friendship to other women in a more altruistic and uplifting form. For example, recent studies reveal in the times of the wagon trains, when the pioneers were crossing from East to West in the United States, women were supporting each other with food and advice to overcome the various obstacles encountered on their journey towards the new frontier. As they changed views of experiences, they also shared recipes and remedies to care for the family. Their organized support made possible the great adventure to conquest the New Frontier. Thus, the comments of experiences among women are not so shallow as it has been characterized through the centuries.

Most of us have not even did not hear of these stories. On the contrary, many of us have grown up hearing that when women gather together, they only speak about fashion or the lives of others. Or, they are only friends with other woman for convenience or for hatching something evil. And that is not the whole truth.

In essence, we must be aware that those "alleged patterns of behavior" should be eradicated for the benefit of society. Undoubtedly there are superficial relationships, but it is not a reason to underestimate the existence and importance of friendship between women. And, one of the big gaps in history has been to precisely ignore and underestimate the relationship and support that always have existed between females.

Intentionally, the rivalry, intrigue, and lack of friendship between women have been systematically documented, but that is only a part of the real history, those stories also occur between men. Additionally, there are also cases of friendship and altruistic female relations where they have put aside personal interest in favor of another female or a group, those stories are not widely circulated.

In order to justify the domination and oppression of women, educational patterns have been developed to perpetuate a negative competition between women. Stories that illustrate negative experiences where the stepmother or the stepsisters are good examples of this destructive behavior. The tale of Cinderella has so many negative prejudices against women. It promotes the concept that women just need to wait for their "prince" to sweep of their feet, and take care of them "forever".

Also, rivalry as the main characteristic in the relations between women has induced them to defeat the achievement of common goals. The presence of a man as a "bone of contention" has been a justification and can complicate matters even more. When a male parent, sibling or lover, is present in the relationship of two women, then those relations can be extremely difficult because it involves competition of who gets the most attention from a man. That is the way in which the majority of women have been educated around the world, although many women are not aware of this pattern.

Lack of sincerity between women is another characteristic, which is difficult to avoid between them. With the excuse of an innocent smile, many females destroy the life of another claiming to be her friend when she distributes a rumor apparently naive and funny. When a woman interacts with another woman it is necessary to be sincere because this implies honesty and simplicity when they deal with each other. There is no excuse to act against this initial attitude, if not, in the end it can tarnish a healthy relationship. Some years ago I thought I had a friend and work colleague. When I asked her for support because of her influential position in order to achieve a job change, she flatly refused and coincidentally used the information I gave her for her own benefit. Months later she called me to invite herself to my house. I had just been married by civil ceremony and I was organizing the religious wedding. Also, during those days my husband's parents were visiting. I explained to my so-called friend I would not be able to entertain her and she was upset because I was destroying her plans to celebrate her birthday at my home. Actually, I did not give importance to the incident. But, 20 years later, by chance I encountered someone who I didn't know but this other woman "was familiar" with the incident. And, to my surprise she had received a completely distorted history of that occurrence. Thus, a person who did not have the real facts concluded that I had acted selfishly when I did not host this so-called friend who I have not seen since that unfortunate incident. Was it a lack of communication? Possibly. What most disturbed me was how easy it was for this so-called friend to alienate me against someone who did not know me, and unfortunately she got a negative image of me without a real reason or justification. The experience serves to illustrate how misleading and irresponsible a friendship can be when it is not mature and respectful. And, of course, always people demand what they don't give.

But, how do we define friendship in the world in which we live?

Gladys Morales-Smith

Friendship is a gift of life. As an old saying goes: " We do not choose our relatives, but we do choose our friends ". And it is so beautiful to trust someone we call friend, despite the time and distance.

Modern life subjects us to constant testing. Either the remoteness or a matter of survival itself many times becomes an excuse to avoid developing ties with our peers. Those ties implicate commitment, solidarity, and spiritual support, which many females are not willing to put in practice. Friendship is a challenge of life, like a flower that requires the warmth of our affections and the sun of openness and loyalty. For me, my sisters, cousins, and other female relatives are first my friends and then my relatives that create a fertile environment and make me value myself and recognize women in general.

The healthy affection, warm and loyal feeling that occurs between two people regardless of their gender is a gift of life. Most women don't know how to cultivate this special feeling because they have been educated with the idea of distrust and competition between same-sex peers, unaware that they have the same concerns, dreams and frustrations. Unfortunately, many women still listen to other women saying that their best friends are men. Nothing wrong with that, but is shows they do not trust another woman. Why many women do not trust each other? Probably it is because they do not make the effort to know themselves and other females.

On the other hand, it is important to recognize that there are women who try to cultivate healthy feelings with other women, which are free from any other interest. True friendship does exist between women, but they are few and far between. There are still remains of competition and lack of sincerity imposed by society that virtually still treat women as minors and impose on them ancestral patterns of behavior. But that is no coincidence. The confrontation between women allows better manipulation of the consciousness of women. When women are more distracted and divided then it is more likely they will not exercise their role as agents for change to create a more harmonious and fair society.

Although friendship between woman and man exists and its benefits are undeniable; this book emphasizes the importance of increasing friendship between women as a way to promote a better environment for everybody.

How can females develop strong friendships?

• Respect and recognize their human essence.

• Appraise and promote the qualities of the other without envy or selfishness.

• Maintain loyalty. Learning how to be truly faithful to another woman is somewhat difficult to practice, but not impossible. Women must be willing to treat others as they want to be treated. If they expect a female friend to be regular and inseparable, sincere and honest, then remember the commitment is mutual.

• To know when to listen and be silent. When women share a secret they have to keep it as their own. Recognize that if they know how to hear at the right time and her friend also will hear them when they need to express their concerns.

To conclude this chapter I transcribe a joke that I found on the Web about the difference of the friendship between people of the same sex:

Friendship between women:

A woman doesn't come home one night and told her husband that she slept at a friend's house. The husband calls 10 of her female friends and they all say: "no she didn't sleep here".

Friendship between men: A man does not sleep one night at his house and told his wife that he stayed at a friend's house. His wife calls 10 of his friends, eight say, " Yes, he slept at their house. Two of them say that he is still with them." (Badboy@ Orble.com)

All jokes exaggerate situations to achieve a smile, and even though the example is not very edifying it, in essence, reflects the general perception about friendship between women which is: lack of commitment, loyalty or sisterhood.

In short, as we see, every culture has developed a form of

friendship between females according to the status of women in their society. This kind of friendship reflects their real progress in terms of implementation and acceptance of them as human beings. It is important to note that, in general there has rarely been written experiences that give models of positive identification in the relationship between women throughout history. And, I would like to see that negative tendency change in the near future for the benefit of society in general.

Chapter 16

Infidelity and the Lack of Loyalty Between Women

The distorted concept of friendship between women reported by the media and throughout history (some of which is true) contributes to conflicting behavior and little loyalty between females, especially when already rivalry is and has been the main ingredient in their relations. Within this vision is perceived the wrong perpetuation of situations justifying the role of women in cases of infidelity. There are stories where a couple suddenly is divorcing because the best friend of a woman falls in love with her friend's husband, who naively reciprocates to the advances of the so-called friend. In fiction, (soap opera or movies) authors try to justify an immoral action describing a hateful and apprehensive wife who is betrayed by a friend who often is described as sweet or more beautiful or younger. All these manipulations in fictitious stories have an actual impact on the every day life of the audience and it is not casual. The old saying of "divide and conquer" continues to be applied. Today, the subject of infidelity in a marriage still is not approached as a problem in the relationship. Most of the time infidelity is "justified" with the presence of a third person, almost always it is the woman who betrays the trust of another woman to achieve her main goal, which is to win the "male trophy". On the other hand is more common that men in similar cases demonstrate more respect tor the existing relationship of a woman to other men.

What few people wonder is, what drives a woman to desire a man already committed in a relationship? Why are mainly women intruders that cause the break up of couples?

In essence, while many men think they are the winners, in reality the unscrupulous women are the ones who purposely ignore how to respect an existing relationship, and they are who ultimately triumph. It is important to recognize and keep in perspective that freedom is an important part of all normal relationships. Also, there are limitations if a person tries to start a new relation with someone who is currently already committed to someone else. Cheating is a moral problem, which is not treated seriously when a woman betrays another woman, because in some way, it has approval from most males. In addition, betrayal between women justifies the old concept of inferiors assigned to females in terms of capacity to cultivate values of self-esteem and respect for their peers.

Gladys Morales-Smith

For this reason, it would be good for many women to remember that in the beginning of a relationship they should ask themselves the following questions:

Is he a free man?

- Does someone like the idea to take a man away from another woman?

- What are the consequences for the female partner if someone has a relationship with a man she already has a wife?

- Can causing suffering to other people (wife, children) in order to "get a man" be called love?

All these considerations are valid in so far as they help us to think about a situation that it is erroneous since its beginning. It is true that no one owns anyone, and no one is forcing anyone into a relationship. But there are also cases where women are looking for committed or married men because it is a challenge, and because also they do not really respect themselves. With the over sexualization of women in the 21st century now the main ingredient to justify infidelity is the lack of sexual understanding of the couple. Thus, the competition game between women takes a new twist to ultimately disguise the old phrase: he'd rather be with me, because... I treat him better; I am better in bed, etc. Those justifications reflect how women continue acting as in the past, without acknowledging their self-respect and respect of their peers. With this interpretation of life, little can be expected to improve society. Unfortunately, a world with infidelity and dysfunctional households, like today, is not a good start for a harmonious and fair society.

Chapter 17

The Mass Media and How it Treats Women

In today's cyber-age women have maintained a questionable place in terms of recognition and integration in society. Although there is substantial progress still we observe patterns of behavior in the mass media designed to increase females roles as sex objects. Another factor is the control of the media by large corporations, which has led to and misrepresented the lack of information on women without any control. The problem is complex and has many economic interests in between which control and manipulation is the issue.

In the last century, women have created positive conditions to protect and encourage their inclusion in society through the media, but they have been isolated efforts. For example, little it has not been commonly known that in the early days of cinema, women from all over the world contributed intellectually to the development of this new art. In the beginning of the 20th century, writers and directors in Hollywood were mostly women. It was with the 1930's depression' and the crisis of the stock market in the Eastern United States where hungry investors turned their eyes to California. There, they displaced the female element from an environment where women's contribution to the industry was already well recognized and accepted in the field. At that time women's' input created another vision of reality in search of a better world. Heroines were real and fashion was a true reflection of what females needed and enjoyed. Unfortunately, that changed when the big production companies were created and with all their advertising technology woman became more objectified than ever.

The situation went from bad to worse and the introduction of television continued to highlight patterns where women were shown as sexual objects as the main role in stories and shows. Therefore Westerns films and television series promoted machismo of their heroes while women played decorative roles and they were generally presented as girls in the "saloon" (cantina) or the selfless wives, ignorant of the outside world.

In the Spanish-speaking countries for example, soap operas proliferated in television with their diminishing effect. Heirs of the famous radio soap operas, this kind of entertainment was used to perpetuate roles that continue to be the distraction of millions of men and women who often applied these behaviors to their reality.

But, this negative phenomenon is a problem around the world.

Still, we can see how today the schedules in the major networks remain with "female times", "female subjects" and includes soap operas that prevail in the programming dedicated to women (mainly afternoon). Even more tragically, today there are proliferating channels completely dedicated to the broadcasting only soap operas. In these real life stories" we see that in a more sophisticated way the media continues promoting behaviors at odds with the times. Spanish networks in the United States offer soap operas, especially from Mexico and Colombia, always tinged with intrigue; the main rivalry between women is to obtain the trophy (man or social recognition) and it is the basic plot of their stories. As a consequence these fictional stories explain how household tangles are moved to the work place, and although it is hard to believe it; these patterns of behavior are transferred to the real life of the viewer and many women (from all socio-economic backgrounds) take them as a way of life. The story of Cinderella is another theme that is repeated and used in a thousand ways and still captures audiences which are ignorant of the subliminal message contained in those programs which are: dependence, submission, and low self-esteem of women who are waiting for a man to "rescue" them.

Rarely seen are stories where women help themselves, or are friends or allies. If they are united (with few exceptions) it is for taking some action against a man or to get benefits, but they do not practice solidarity as an intrinsic value of their gender.

Between Women, Friends or Enemies?

How this negative influence from the mainstream mass media should be controlled? It is difficult to give recipes to stop the avalanche of misinformation and manipulation of them. The presence of female characters ignoring the human essence of women and how they become icons for new generations is an issue that deserves attention. For example the television show "Playboy" which was broadcast only for a short period of time, because of the protest of feminists like Gloria Steinem. The show was trying to give a sexual idealized concept of girls working at the Playboy's clubs.

If the mass media is evaluated as to how it portrays the image of women today, it shows there is a mixture of super sexualization and a kind of super heroine capable of doing everything and anything to achieve their purposes. Women are portrayed as being able to have it all, job, family, money, etc. And, this female prototype does not know or practice realistic lifestyle and goals with unobtainable objectives. But, this prototype is not exclusively a product of a given mass media, with slight differences between them; this kind of model is consider as the real ideal of women in the 21st century.

In this sense, information and propagation of moral values through non-conventional media, for example social networks, is an alternative to counteract this avalanche of damage that is destroying the very foundations of society as a whole.

What is it the role of realistic behavior, good manners and

proper moral choices in this context? Harmonious relations will allow the dissemination of information regarding the importance of creating linkages for a better and more just society. If women treat themselves better, a current of self-esteem and respect will make them stronger as a group in society.

It is advisable to suggest certain attitudes that could help to stop this aggressive trend against females in the media:

• Denounce and dismiss the promotion, either as an audience or as a participant, of events, which denigrate the person in order to have a trophy, or for a few moments of attention. That is the case of reality shows, talk shows and some beauty pageants where mainly the non-conscious women are the main attraction.

• Question characters and programs at odds with the human condition including ones promoting the increase of infamous contests, talk shows or reality shows. Also, omit programs showcasing demeaning humor, which only invites the denigration of human beings. We can see how the possession of low self-esteem and desire of a minute of fame motivates many young people (men and women) to expose their lower instincts as human beings in order to stay longer or showcase themselves on a program. Thus we see women treated as sexual objects, behavior which provides an example for imitation among people hungry for alternative patterns of behavior. Hence, they imitate what they believe is accepted and popular.

• Justifying female denigration the media have historically portrayed women and other minorities as inferiors and unable to defend themselves or incapable to earn a place of respect in society. Despite laws and developments of the past 50 years, there are still groups of females where progress has not reached them; and such reality, movies and talk shows, etc., programs are often directed to this kind of female population.

• Monitor the media' use of aggression towards each other as a resource that is used by the media in recent times. Added to the subtle use of aggressiveness as a defense for the victim many times this type of action influences all kinds of audiences. And usually the reaction is not so positive or sympathetic.

• Watch women at the very basic human levels in the media attempt to any kind of respect to other humans and also to oneself.

• Looking at themselves with respect, women can make more difficult for the media to abuse and denigrate them. And, we cannot forget those who unscrupulously are living at the expense of denigration not only from women but also from people in general, many of them are in the mass media circle.

• Caring for themselves and recognizing the value of other females, it will not be so easy to proliferate programs or any organization, which perpetuates their exclusion in society. Besides laws, quotas and thousands of rules in favor of women, females themselves need to know and practice them, in order to overcome their unequal situation in society.

CHAPTER 18

Relationships Between Women from Ethno-Cultural Minorities

According to my observations, women are much more discriminatory than men, especially when it comes to different cultures. In spite of the fact that there is a greater multiculturalism in the social spectrum of the 21st Century, there still exist bigoted and racial individuals, including women, who play a decisive role in perpetuating discrimination regardless of their origin.

Recently, I had the opportunity to talk with a female sales associate in a chain of stores in the United States. The woman was of Mexican origin and when I saw people waiting in big lines at the cash register, I asked her about the lack of staff. She informed me that since a "Latina" supervisor had been put in charge, she asked them to work harder and did not emphasize proper verbal manners. According to my source, this "Latina" manager had a negative attitude toward other workers from the same cultural origin. Also, she required sales associates, especially "Latinos", to perform work unrelated to their contracts such as cleaning floors or bathrooms. The new supervisor did not respect their clerks' qualifications and underestimated them. Although the general management had offered her to increase her staff, this supervisor said that it was not necessary and expressed her feeling that "Latinos" are usually idle and it was necessary to make them work.

Personally, I have had negative experiences with women belonging to different minorities. I remember working in a government office in California, and at that time I had the opportunity to observe on existing prejudices among "Latinos" themselves including women from other minorities. Relations were not easy and created a very difficult working environment.

Unfortunately, this is a small example of the lack of solidarity among minorities and especially between women. Particularly when a woman from a minority group reaches a position of power, then her insecurities, frustrations, and lack of social awareness results in contempt for her own ethnic group.

In essence, it is the lack of recognition and respect of some women themselves that makes them look down upon their pears, regardless of gender or ethnic origin. Of course, it is worse when they both belong to disadvantaged groups and have limited skills to integrate into society.

This subject is very broad and requires a thorough study. Also, the solution is not only to offer laws of protection as a framework of reference, because, on the other hand, there is a possible abuse of those provisions by minority groups themselves. Such is the case, for example, in the United States of the so-called "Affirmative Action Law" which in the past allowed African Americans and immigrants, including Spanish speaking individuals, (mostly Cubans and Mexicans) to have quotas at universities and government work places. Unfortunately, some of these same beneficiaries became enemies of their own groups. For example, some of the beneficiaries of this law maintained the prejudices that they were once victims of, and used those bigotries against their minority peers. Thus, the supposed beneficiaries used negatively a law that was created to give minorities more equality. Many beneficiaries of the Affirmative Action Law, who were from Hispanic origin, sarcastically are called "coconuts" (Brown on the outside, white on the inside). They usually are people born in the United States, with low income and from parents with minimal education, who project the limitations of their origins to the new waves of immigrants. Many "Latina" women fit this description.

On the other hand, it is good to remember that women from minority groups using the justification of survival forget their roots and become channels of the perpetuation of discrimination and injustice. Eradicating this behavior is a common challenge. It is difficult to find solutions because the dynamics of society as a whole does not allow a change, especially with minorities. A possible good start is to establish educational programs where tolerance and positive self-esteem is taught as a basic requirement to promote better treatment among women from the same ethno-cultural groups. The revaluation of their minority traditions, without exaggeration or chauvinism is urgent. Also, it is necessary to provide special education throughout society to the new generations regarding their ethnic origins so they can see themselves with respect, solidarity, and recognition. With this practice, we can expect a change of consciousness that allows a better treatment between females of the same immigrant group.

In the specific case of the United States, the existence of Spanish television networks which perpetuate models of behavior incompatible with the advancement of women are a major obstacle to the achievement of greater integration of the Hispanic women, into the American society. As long as these entities maintain programs with patterns of self-discrimination and relegation of the Hispanic sector, most Hispanic females will be negatively influenced and maintain a disadvantaged position in society. In other words, the proliferation of radio stations, television channels and news sources (printed or digital) used by many minorities as a media liaison are poorly utilized by those media producers, and only serve to isolate more the minority groups who look to them for help.

Gladys Morales-Smith

In countries like the United States or Europe, foreign communities especially from Latin America are holding back their acceptance to the main stream when they only rely on these kinds of media sources. As a consequence, they have caused more damage than benefit. In other words, minority media has deepened the differences of the minority groups, perpetuating their irreparable isolation. Hence minorities groups should be aware that these channels are only entertainment, because there are also limitations and repercussions into this kind of media. Real life is not represented accurately in the minority mass media and it is good to remember that formal education is the key to teaching all people respect and solidarity for each other.

CHAPTER 19

Inter- Generational Treatment Between Women

The relationship between women most of the time is difficult due to external pressure in society. Also, when there are not specific parameters of behavior between them, their relation is more complicated, especially when women from different generations meet in any circumstance of life.

Often if a woman is older, she believes she has the key for all the answers and minimizes the ability of the younger ones. And, if the young person wants to stand out then she belittles and diminishes the qualities of more mature woman. On the other hand, an aging traditional woman can no longer use her body and beauty to attract attention and support as she could when she was younger. It does not occur in all cases, but it is a generality. The fact is that if their relationships are based on traditional patterns of external appearance including rivalry and lack of loyalty then, those women easily will fall into confrontation with each other.

Questions that many women should ask themselves include: Who is younger and more attractive? Who offers more to the senses in moments of pleasure? Those immediate considerations are still used to establish a pattern of discriminatory and harmful relations, which creates a lack of respect between females, especially from different ages.

Aging with dignity and grace is a challenge for everyone, regardless of his or her gender. Today, scientific advancements allow a greater life expectancy and thus the boundaries of the past have been widely surpassed. Thus we see people over sixty actively in the labor force, and many times they often exceed seventy years of age, and they are still active and vital individuals.

All these changes of recent decades have generated new perspectives in terms of the way women behave. In a society where often the external appearance is more important for women than men this attitude creates frustrations and negative reactions, which are reflected when, aging women are dealing with their peers or younger females. This more increasingly cruel and elemental practice can be avoided. Creating awareness among the young people that life has different cycles of which no one is exempt. It is essential in this sense, that new generations who learn ways to live better, also should be taught how to grow old gracefully and respect the older generations. It is good to keep in mind that to a greater or lesser extent from the moment of birth all of us age as a natural part of the lives of everyone.

In essence, the key for women to fairly treat each other is respect. People must recognize the wisdom that comes with gray hair and the enthusiasm of youth as a basis for successful relationships between generations of women. Many times women demand of young people what they do not offer to them.

It is good to remember that plastic surgery does not erase years, it only delays the cosmetic effects of them. In addition, it is an option but not an obligation. For example, Sally Field, (American actress) in a recent interview said that she would not use plastic surgery despite the fact that she did not like the look of her neck. She has passed the barrier of 60 and she appears naturally beautiful. Julia Roberts has also joined the group of movie stars who dispute plastic surgery as a way to slow the passage of the years, because it is not natural and is against our human essence. The laudable viewpoint of these icons is good to take into consideration because they are giving messages against a practice that ultimately distorts our reality.

It is important to remember:

• To be older does not give someone the license to do anything because of his or her age.

• To be young does not mean a person is better and has more to offer.

Gladys Morales-Smith

• To be young does not mean a person has more rights, because the older already have lived, and often have more wisdom that comes with living longer. While we are alive and have the wish for a better world, everyone should be committed to act as better human beings and contribute with her or his behavior to a more harmonious and just world. Age should not be an obstacle, but a bridge.

Final Thoughts

For centuries women have been divided spiritually. Ignorance, limitations of language, lack of education, and communication still there are always thousands of reasons, which bring a single result: they were and continue being relegated to integrate into society. These ancestral limitations have serious consequences either in the so-called industrialized countries or the less developed ones where women do not comply with their role as agent for change. Many individual cases of recognition are virtually erased given the amount of denigrated and forgotten women.

It is not time for lamentations, we must be aware that the biggest change should emerge from ourselves. Appreciating ourselves with the recognition that all women are human beings with different visions of life, but with the common desire that future generations of women contribute positively to a better world is the best way to eradicate errors from the past.

Gladys Morales-Smith

The existence of laws to protect women are no guarantee of a qualitative change in today's society, the change comes from within us. With higher self-esteem, women will respect their peers and themselves. Furthermore, equal education, without discrimination of sex or ethnicity is a basic requirement for an ideal behavior where the legal framework is real and not a picture of embellishment for demagogic use by mediocre and incompetent politicians.

Respect comes from within. When treatment between women is equal, with courtesy and appropriate language then we can say that we are going in the right direction. The importance of how women treat themselves is vital, without forgetting that they are part of a whole and that men must also learn to include them as equals. That will be possible if women contribute with gentle and supportive behavior themselves. The practice of solidarity between women is a key component in these efforts. We must not forget that kindness does not speak of sex. A world without domination of one sex or the other will ensure fair societies. If we respect ourselves, if we contribute to harmonious societies and remind ourselves that love for our fellows human beings is universal, then progress will be made for all people.

Annex 1.

"Guidelines on Gender-Neutral Language" (Published by United Nations for Education, Science and Culture, UNESCO)

Examples of phrasing: Ambiguity

Example:

1. Man's search for knowledge has led him to improve scientific methodology.

Alternative:

The search for knowledge has led us to improve scientific methodology.

Comment:

Rephrased, using first person.

Alternative:

People have continually sought knowledge.

Comment:

Rewritten in two sentences.

Alternative:

The search for knowledge has led to improvements in scientific methodology.

Comment:

Rephrased, leaving the agent implicit.

Example:

2. The use of experiments in psychology presupposes the mechanistic nature of man.

Alternative:

The use of experiments in psychology presupposes the mechanistic nature of the human being.

Comment:

Noun substituted.

Example:

3. Man, mankind

Between Women, Friends or Enemies?

Alternative:

People, humanity, human beings, humankind, the human species, the human race, we, ourselves, men and women, homo sapiens, one, the

public, society, the self, human nature.

Comment:

In this group of examples a variety of terms may be substituted.

Example:

Man's achievements.

Alternative:

Human achievements, achievements of the human species, achievement of our ancestors.

Example:

The average man, man in the street.

Alternative:

The average person/individual, people in general, one.

Example:

Primitive man

Alternative:

Primitive people or peoples, primitive human beings, primitive men and women.

Example:

To man (a project, etc.)

Alternative:

To staff (a Project), hire personnel, employ staff, operate, run, administer.

Example:

Manfully

Alternative:

Valiantly.

Example:

Committee of wise men

Between Women, Friends or Enemies?

Alternative:

Committee/panel of counselors, eminent persons, advisory panel.

Example:

"Man and the Biosphere" (program)

Comment:

Existing titles of programs, documents, etc. cannot as a rule be changed, but it is advisable to avoid generic man in new titles.

Example:

'History of the Scientific and Cultural Development of Mankind'

Alternative:

'History of Humanity'

Comments:

This has been the official title since 1992.

Manning table

Alternative:

Staffing table

Example:

Manpower

Alternative:

Staff, labor, work force, employees, personnel, workers, human resources, human power, and human energy.

Example:

Man-made

Alternative:

Artificial, synthetic, manufactured, of human construction, of human origin, human-induced, techno genic, machine-made.

Comment:

The appropriate term will depend on the context (avoid man-made unless males alone are involved)

Example:

Brotherhood of man

Between Women, Friends or Enemies?

Alternative:

Human fellowship, human kinship, solidarity

Example:

Brotherly.

Alternative:

Comradely, friendly, co-operative

Example:

Man and wife.

Alternative:

Husband and wife, wife and husband

Example:

Man-months

Alternative:

Work-months, staff-months.

Example:

Businessman

Alternative:

Business manager, executive, head of firm, agent, representative, business traveler; (Pl.) business community, business people.

Example:

Cameraman

Alternative:

Photographer, camera operator; (Pl.) camera crew

Example:

Caveman

Alternative:

Cave dweller

Example:

Chairman

Alternative:

Between Women, Friends or Enemies?

Chairperson, chair, president, presiding officer

Example:

Craftsman

Alternative:

Craft worker, artisan, craftsperson; (Pl.) craftspeople.

Example:

Craftsmanship.

Alternative:

Craft, craft skills.

Example:

Draughtsman (British) Draftsman (EEUU)

Alternative:

Designer

Example:

Fellow countryman

Alternative:

Compatriot

Example:

Fireman

Alternative:

Fire-fighter; (Pl.) fire crew, fire brigade

Example:

Foreman

Alternative:

Supervisor, superintendent

Example:

Gentleman's agreement

Alternative:

Honorable agreement

Example:

Landlord

Between Women, Friends or Enemies?

Alternative:

Owner, proprietor

Example:

Layman

Alternative:

Layperson, non-specialist, non-professional, novice.

Example:

Ombudsman

Alternative:

Mediator

Example:

Policeman/men

Alternative:

Police officer, or (PL) just police. 'John Smith is a policeman' but 'it is the duty of every police officer...'

Example:

Salesman/girl

Alternative:

Shop assistant, sales assistant, shop worker; (Pl.) sales staff.

Example:

Spokesman

Alternative:

Spokesperson, representative, official. 'Ms. X was the spokeswoman' but "The delegation shall appoint a spokesperson/representative', etc.

Comment:

Use spokesman or spokeswoman as appropriate when a specific person is intended. Use non gender-specific term when reference is indeterminate, i.e. to post or function. This applies to '-man' terms generally.

Example:

Sportsman

Alternative:

Athlete, sportsman/sportswoman

Between Women, Friends or Enemies?

Example:

Statesman

Alternative:

Political leader, stateswoman (where appropriate), public servant

Example:

Statesmanship

Alternative:

Statecraft

Example:

Workmanlike

Alternative:

Serviceable, well-made, well executed, skillful

Example:

4. The teacher is usually appointed on the basis of his training.

Alternative:

Teachers are usually appointed on the basis of their training.

Comment:

Changed to plural.

Example:

5. The learner should not be cut off from his roots; his own culture and traditions should be respected.

Alternative:

Learners should not be cut off from their roots; their own culture and traditions should be respected.

Comments:

Rewritten in plural.

Example:

6. The individual is strongly influenced by his family's values.

Alternative:

As individuals, we are strongly influenced by our family's values.

Between Women, Friends or Enemies?

Comment:

Pronoun substituted, his omitted.

Example:

7. There were 16 girls and 16 boys in the class. Each child was to write an essay on his favorite hobby.

Alternative:

Each child was to write an essay on his or her favorite hobby.

Comment:

Change his to his or her; however, use sparingly to avoid monotonous repetition.

Example:

8. Anyone disagreeing with this statement should give his reasons.

Alternative:

All those disagreeing with this statement should give their reasons.

Comment:

Another possibility would be 'Anyone...should give their reasons', since use of they as a singular pronoun of common gender is widely used and has sound historical antecedents.

Examples of phrasing: Stereotyping

Example:

1.This woman's husband lets her work part-time

Alternative:

This woman's husband 'lets' her work part-time

Comment:

Punctuation added to clarify location of the bias, that is, with husband and wife, not with author. The word 'sic' may also be inserted. Always consider the context. In some cases the example quoted may literally accurate.

Alternative:

The husband says he 'lets' his wife work part-time.

Comment:

If necessary, rewrite to clarify as allegation.

Alternative:

Between Women, Friends or Enemies?

This woman works part-time

Comment:

The author of the example quoted intended to communicate the working status of the woman but inadvertently revealed a stereotype about husband-wife relationships.

Example:

2.John and Mary both have full-time jobs; he helps her with the housework.

Alternative:

...They share the housework

Comment:

The example quoted implies that housework is a duty for a woman, optional for a man. The alternative is still comprehensive enough to designate a traditional situation, since it does not imply that they necessarily share equally. Whether they do can be made clear by the context.

Example:

3. Research scientists often neglect their wives and children.

Alternative:

Research scientists often neglect their families.

Comment:

Alternative wording acknowledges that women as well as men are research scientists.

Example:

4.Transport will be provided for delegates and their wives.

Alternatives:

Transport will be provided for delegates and their spouses or person accompanying them.

Example:

5. The survey shows that Americans of higher status are less likely to have fat wives.

Alternative:

The survey shows that American men of higher status are less likely to have fat wives.

Example:

Between Women, Friends or Enemies?

6. The doctor...he

Alternative:

Doctors... they; the doctor...she

Comment:

Be specific. Change to plural if discussing women as well as men or use he/she (the form 's/he' may be used in moderation).

Example:

7. The nurse...she

Alternative:

Nurses...they; the nurse... he

Example:

8. Woman doctor, male nurse

Alternative:

Doctor, nurse.

Comment:

Specify sex if sex indication is relevant to the context.

Example:

9. Mothering

Alternative:

Parenting, nurturing, child-rearing, childcare, affection (or specify exact behavior); mollycoddling, fussing (if pejorative sense is intended)

Comment:

Noun substituted. Fathering, in addition to its sense of an act of procreation, now has a meaning parallel to mothering.

Example:

10. Men and girls.

Alternative:

Men and women, women and men.

Comment:

Use parallel terms. Of course use men and girls if that is literally what is meant. In casual use, girl is acceptable as parallel to guy/bloke/chap, etc. (In the United States, guy may refer to both sexes).

Between Women, Friends or Enemies?

Example:

Girl

Alternative:

Woman

Comment:

Use woman if reference is to an adult.

Example:

Girls

Alternative:

Acknowledge their status, whether secretaries, typists, keyboard operators, office assistants, a team, etc.

Comment:

All of these may also be male.

Example:

11. Housewife

Alternative:

Homemaker, consumer, customer, shopper, 'housewife'.

Comment:

Be specific according to context. The person designated need not be female.

Example:

12. Lady

Alternative:

Woman

Comment:

Use lady only as a parallel to gentleman.

Example:

13. Emasculated

Alternative:

Weakened, enfeebled, diminished, toothless, tame, and watered-down.

Example:

14. Effeminate.

Alternative:

Delicate, feeble, fussy, soft, languid, affected, gentle.

Example:

15. Ambitious men but aggressive woman

Alternative:

Ambitious women, men, people, individuals; aggressive individuals, people, women, men.

Comment:

Some adjectives, depending on whether the person described is a man or a women, connote bias. The examples illustrate some common usages that may not always convey exact meaning, especially when paired as in examples 15.

Example:

Cautious men but timid women

Alternative:

Cautious men, women, people, individuals; timid people,

men, women, individuals.

Example:

Outspoken men but strident/shrill women

Alternative:

Outspoken individuals, women, men, people; strident/shrill men, women, people, individuals.

Example:

Emotional men but hysterical women.

Alternative:

Emotional men, women, people, individuals.

Comment:

Use of the word hysterical originated in the belief that the uterus moved around the body, causing women to behave strangely.

Examples:

16. Forefathers

Alternative:

Between Women, Friends or Enemies?

Ancestors, forebears

Example:

17. Founding fathers

Alternative:

Founders.

Example:

18. The student's behavior was typically female.

Alternative:

The student's behavior was.. (Specify)

Comment:

Being specific reduces possibility of stereotype bias.

Example:

19. Authoress

Alternative:

Author

Comment:

Avoid " ess" wherever possible. It is often pejorative or perceived as such.

Example:

Poetess

Alternative:

Poet

Example:

Steward/stewardess

Alternative:

Flight attendant; (Pl.) cabin crew

Example:

20. Tomboy

Alternative:

Intrepid child, boisterous child

Example:

Between Women, Friends or Enemies?

21. Woman driver

Alternative:

Driver.

Examples of phrasing: Titles and forms of address

Example:

1.Mr. and Mrs. John Smith

Alternative:

Jane and John Smith, Mr. and Mrs. Smith, Mr. and Ms. Smith

Comment: In the example 1, the wife's identity has been wholly absorbed by her husband's.

Example:

2. Miss, Mrs.

Alternative:

Ms.

Comment:

If possible, ascertain which courtesy title the woman herself prefers, otherwise use Ms. (of which the accepted plural is Mesdames). A woman's marital status is very often irrelevant to the matter in hand (participation in a meeting, etc.) and there is no masculine equivalent of Miss/Mrs.

Example:

3. Chairman

Alternative:

Chairperson, chair, president, presiding officer. When addressing the individual: Madam Chairperson, Mr. Chairperson.

Comment.- When new bodies are set up or rules of procedure, etc. of existing bodies are updated, chairperson, chair of president should be used in place of chairman.

Bibliography

"Etiquette. The Blue Book of Social usage", Emily Post (1922)

"Revolution from Within. A Book of Self-Esteem", Gloria Steinem.(1991)

"The American Sisterhood", Wendy Martin (1972)

"The Second Sex". Simone de Beauvoir (1948).

"Simone de Beauvoir, A Biography". Deirdre Bair (1990).

"Heart Thinking, Counterpoint of Friendship Between Women", Elaine Audet (2000).

"Man made language," Dale Spender (1980)."Linguistic sexism.

Analysis and Proposals to Sexual Discrimination in Language". Calero M.A. Fernández (1999)

"Ideology Sexist and Language". A.V. Cátala González and e. Garcia Pascual (1995)

"The Sexist Language in the Media". Susana Guerrero Salazar (2002)

"Towards a non Sexist Language in digital communication". Susana Guerrero Salazar (2011)

Gladys Morales-Smith

Links

http://www.onlinewomeninpolitics.org

http://www.womeninworldhistory.org

http://www.Fordham.edu/halsall/women/womensbook/asp

http://www.Feminism.eserver.org

http://www.essortment.com/history_etiquette

http://www.en.wikipedia.org/wikie/gender_neutrality_in_English

http://www.Rae.es

http://www.unesdoc.unesco.org

http://www.sisyphe.org

Between Women, Friends or Enemies?

About the author:

Gladys Morales-Smith was born in Lima, Peru. A journalist by vocation and with an academic education in the mass media field, she has practiced the art of writing in Spanish for the majority of the last several decades. She also as a diplomat has worked in many Latin American countries, and in the United States of America. In addition, she holds a Bachelor's Degree in International Relations, and Postgraduate courses in Sociology and International Business.

Her interest in women's issues dates back to the 1970s. At that time in Peru, (for the first time thanks to the socialization of newspapers) the papers contained a section dedicated to highlight the values and achievements of Peruvian women. The traditional social page was replaced by one dedicated to publicize the intellectual side of women, a difficult task, which with time and due to traditional political interests began fading in 1980 with new rules and restrictions. The seed for being interested in women's' issues continued to grow within Gladys. Thus the interest and journalistic curiosity of the author turned into searching for answers to many years of relegation and disappointment of the role of women in modern society. After nearly four decades of interest and experience the issue is more complex than ever. The present book is published as a result of the accumulated knowledge of the author on women's issues and her desire to contribute with solutions to a situation where women are still behind a real progress, which is a better treatment between females.

It is the hope of the author that through education and an increase of women's' self-awareness and confidence females will be able to continue to contribute in a positive manner for better changes in society.